Mark Twain & The Bible

MARK TWAIN

& THE BIBLE

Allison Ensor

UNIVERSITY OF KENTUCKY PRESS

TO
Anne
&
Beth

Acknowledgments

THIS BOOK could not have been what it is without the assistance of several persons whose help I gratefully acknowledge: Professor Edwin H. Cady, Indiana University, guided me through the preliminaries of this study; Professor Nathalia Wright, University of Tennessee, whose study of Melville and the Bible is still a standard work, read my manuscript and made valuable suggestions; Professor Henry Nash Smith, University of California at Berkeley, former editor of the Mark Twain Papers, read an earlier version of the book and encouraged and directed me by his comments on it; the Graduate School of the University of Tennessee awarded me a summer grant, releasing me from teaching responsibilities for a term so that I might revise the manuscript; and my wife, Anne Lovell Ensor, was willing to accept Mark Twain as a member of the family for some five years.

Contents

ABBREVIATIONS USED IN THE TEXT

Biography	Albert Bigelow Paine, *Mark Twain: A Biography*. New York, 1912.
Complete Essays	*The Complete Essays of Mark Twain*, ed. Charles Neider. Garden City, N.Y., 1963.
Complete Short Stories	*The Complete Short Stories of Mark Twain*, ed. Charles Neider. Garden City, N.Y., 1957.
Eruption	*Mark Twain in Eruption*, ed. Bernard DeVoto. New York, 1940.
Europe	*Europe and Elsewhere*, ed. Albert Bigelow Paine. New York, 1923.
Forgotten Writings	*The Forgotten Writings of Mark Twain*, ed. Henry Duskis. New York, 1963.
Johnson	Merle Johnson, *A Bibliography of Mark Twain*. New York, 1935.
Letters	*Mark Twain's Letters*, ed. Albert Bigelow Paine. New York, 1917.
LE	*Letters from the Earth*, ed. Bernard DeVoto. New York, 1962.
Letters from Hawaii	*Mark Twain's Letters from Hawaii*, ed. A. Grove Day. New York, 1966.
Love Letters	*The Love Letters of Mark Twain*, ed. Dixon Wecter. New York, 1949.
Mrs. Fairbanks	*Mark Twain to Mrs. Fairbanks*, ed. Dixon Wecter. San Marino, Calif., 1949.
My Father	Clara Clemens, *My Father, Mark Twain*. New York, 1931.
Notebook	*Mark Twain's Notebook*, ed. Albert Bigelow Paine. New York, 1935.
"Reflections"	"Reflections on Religion," ed. Charles Neider. *Hudson Review*, XVI (Autumn, 1963), 329–52.
Report from Paradise	*Report from Paradise*, ed. Dixon Wecter. New York, 1952.
Satires and Burlesques	*Mark Twain's Satires and Burlesques*, ed. Franklin R. Rogers. Berkeley and Los Angeles, 1967.
Speeches	*Mark Twain's Speeches*, ed. Albert Bigelow Paine. New York, 1923.
Traveling	*Traveling with the Innocents Abroad*, ed. Daniel M. McKeithan. Norman, Okla., 1958.
Travels with Mr. Brown	*Mark Twain's Travels with Mr. Brown*, ed. Franklin Walker and G. Ezra Dane. New York, 1940.
Twain-Howells Letters	*Mark Twain-Howells Letters*, ed. Henry Nash Smith and William M. Gibson. Cambridge, Mass., 1960.
Twain's Autobiography	*Mark Twain's Autobiography*, ed. Albert Bigelow Paine. New York, 1924.
Writings	*The Writings of Mark Twain*, Author's National Edition. New York, 1907–1918.

I.

The Writer & The Bible

Mark twain once claimed that at the age of two weeks he knew the Bible well enough to protest being named Samuel after a boy whom the Lord "had to call ... a couple of times before he would come!"[1] If that was, as Huck Finn would say, "a stretcher," it is true that Samuel Clemens came to know the Bible early and that it exerted a powerful influence upon him all his life. There are those who love the Bible, those who hate it, and still others who simply ignore it. Twain raged against it as wicked, obscene, and damnatory; but he could never ignore it. "At last he threw out the Bible," Edgar Lee Masters said of him, "but it seemed to be attached to a rubber band, and was likely to bounce back into his lap at any time. The mythology of Christianity engrossed his imagination." "All his epigrams and dialectics," he concluded, "are directed against fables that are not worth noticing."[2] Fable or not, Twain was truly caught up in the Bible. And the dialectic of rejection and attraction, of throwing it out only to have it bounce back, was lifelong.

It has often been recognized that Twain was more influenced by the Bible than by any other book and that he drew upon it uniquely for ideas, subjects, and imagery.[3] He read it through while still in his teens and dipped into it with varying intensities from that time on. During two periods of his life he made extensive use of it: in his *Quaker City* excursion to the Holy Land and his courtship of Olivia Langdon, roughly 1867–1870, and in the final years of his life, approximately 1893–1909, when biblical fantasies and criticism flowed freely from his pen.

There are many different ways in which Twain used the Bible. A reference may consist only of the name of a biblical character in a strictly nonbiblical context; or, at the opposite extreme, it may be a lengthy direct quotation. An allusion may be identified by chapter and verse; more often there is no indication whatever that the Bible is being quoted. A biblical character may be named for no other purpose than to suggest some particular quality with which that character is commonly associated (wisdom, Solomon; antiquity, Methuselah); or Twain may build an entire sketch or even a small book around biblical characters and incidents. He may use the Bible quite seriously and reverently; or it may serve him as a source of humor. He may parody, ridicule, or—particularly in his later years—revile it. Its characters, incidents, and phrasing came readily— though not always accurately—to hand whenever he had need of them.

Twain's choice of biblical subjects was partly dictated by his own background. He had lived in a community where many people revered the Bible as the Word of God, as virtually a letter direct from the hand of the Almighty. He believed that most Christians still regarded the Bible with awe and took its statements as literal truth.[4] Furthermore, he thought that most Americans, whether Christian or not, knew the Bible stories fairly well—certainly better than any other literature. Thus the Bible provided a common ground on which Twain and his audience could meet. Sam Clemens became acquainted with the Bible early in life, particularly through the efforts of his mother and his sister Pamela. As he recalled it many years later, "the unfaithful guardians of my young life ... not only permitted but compelled me to read an unexpurgated Bible through before I was 15 years old."[5] At Sam's Sunday school, as at Tom Sawyer's, great emphasis was placed on memorizing Bible verses. To provide the children with an incentive, certain rewards were instituted, though the system at the little church Sam attended was less complex than that described in *Tom Sawyer*. A blue ticket could be obtained by reciting two verses, while five would bring three blue tickets and the privilege of borrowing a book from the Sunday school library for one week. The books were in all probability the kind he was to satirize in "The Story of the Good Little Boy" and "The Story of the Bad Little Boy," but Sam wanted the privilege anyway. Like Tom, he contrived to get it without work, though in a different manner: according to his autobiography, he simply recited the same five verses— from the parable of the wise and foolish virgins—every Sunday, and his teacher never seemed to be aware that he had heard them from the same person before.[6]

Twain never systematically recorded what he studied in Sunday school or stated what stories appealed to him most. Such information has to be gathered from here and there in his vast writings, but there is enough of it to show that he was strongly impressed by some of what he read and heard. We know that he, like Tom, who supposed that a United States senator would be twenty-five feet tall,[7] imagined everything in the Bible stories as being on a scale far grander than reality. According to his 1867 letters from the Holy Land, he thought as a boy that the Jordan River was four thousand miles long and thirty-five miles wide and that the Sea of Galilee was sixty thousand miles in diameter.[8] When he read phrases like "all these kings" in Joshua 11:5 and elsewhere, he imagined a group comparable to a gathering of the kings of England, France, Spain, Germany, and Russia, instead of what he would later call "a parcel of petty chiefs—ill-clad and ill-conditioned savages" whose kingdoms were perhaps five miles square and contained two thousand people (*Writings*, II, 239). No doubt part of his disgust with the Holy Land was caused by the exaggerated pictures of conditions there he had formed in youth. Piecing together various statements, we can say that in Sunday school Sam studied the wise and foolish virgins,[9] the raising of Lazarus,[10] the spying expedition in the land of Canaan,[11] the Prodigal Son,[12] and the fall of Adam and Eve.[13] Of course Sam must have heard about and seen pictures of a good many other biblical events such as the flood, the crossing of the Red Sea, David's slaying Goliath, and the life of Jesus. Sermons, too—much more Bible-based than many delivered today—tended to impress deeply upon the boy's mind the striking events of Scripture. Dixon Wecter has summed up what Twain inherited from his early biblical training: "the will to disbelieve, but also a lifelong fascination with the mythology taught."[14] There we have it: the will to disbelieve, a lifelong fascination. These are the elements that play back and forth in Twain's attitude toward the Bible from that time on.

With the kind of training he had and his almost instinctive liking for biblical subjects, it seems natural enough that when he began writing for his brother

Orion's Hannibal *Journal* Sam Clemens drew upon the Bible for some of his material. Most references were minor; the one extended Bible-based passage in his work for that paper was an 1852 discourse upon the virtue of having red hair: "Thomas Jefferson's hair was red—and Jesus Christ, our Savior—'The chief among ten thousand, and altogether lovely,' is said to have had auburn hair—and, although it is not stated in so many words, I have but little doubt that Adam's hair was red—for he was made of 'red earth' (as his name indicates); and as the name Adam was given to him *after* he was made, it is pretty clear he must have had red hair! And the great probability is that Eve's hair was red also, she being made of a 'rib' from Adam, who was made of a lump of 'red earth.' Now Adam and Eve before they sinned, are generally supposed to have been the most lovely and beautiful of creation, and they, in all probability were both 'red headed.' "[15]

Besides demonstrating Sam's attraction to Adam, the biblical character he was to use more than any other in his future works, this passage shows that he was willing to be a little free with the personages of the Bible, even with Jesus Christ, though he speaks of him reverently. It also demonstrates that Sam knew more about the Bible than just its text. The phrase from the Song of Solomon used to describe Christ is evidence that he knew the official interpretation of such passages, that the book is an allegory of the love of Christ for the Church. That he had been exposed to biblical exegesis appears from his connecting the name "Adam" with the earth.

In the following year we find Sam employing the Bible in a newspaper letter criticizing a St. Louis minister. Of a destitute widow and her five children, he writes: "The sight brought to mind the handsome sum our preacher collected in church last Sunday to obtain food and raiment for the poor, ignorant heathen in some far off part of the world; I thought, too, of the passage in the Bible instructing the disciples to carry their good works into all the world—*beginning first at Jerusalem.*"[16] This one passage contains many characteristics which Twain's use of the Bible continued to manifest for the remainder of his life: introduction of brief biblical phrases, citation of a biblical passage with brief quotation from that passage, quotation slightly altered from the Bible's wording, and use of the Bible to criticize the insufficiently Christian representatives of Christianity. The passage cited is Luke 24:27, but Sam's zeal supplied a word not in the Bible, which has simply, "beginning at Jerusalem." The phrase "food and raiment" is also biblical, appearing in Deuteronomy 10:18, I Timothy 6:8 and elsewhere.

More personal is a letter to his sister-in-law, written in 1858, when the steamboat *Pennsylvania* exploded sixty miles below Memphis, fatally injuring his younger brother Henry: "Hardened, hopeless,—aye, lost—lost —lost and ruined sinner as I am—*I, even I,* have humbled myself to the ground and prayed as never man prayed before, that the great God might let this cup pass from me—that he would strike me to the earth, but spare my brother. ... Men take me by the hand and *congratulate* me, and call me 'lucky' because I was not on the Pennsylvania when she blew up! May God forgive them, for they know not what they say."[17] It must be obvious from this passage that Sam no longer considered himself a Christian. And yet, biblical language came so readily to him that he repeated as his own two prayers which Jesus had uttered in the moments of his greatest agony, at Gethsemane and Calvary.

That Clemens was quite unorthodox in his religious thought by the time of his departure for Nevada in 1861 did not mean that he had forgotten his experiences with the Bible at home, school, and church. What it did mean was that he had greater freedom to use the Bible as he chose, and he frequently did it in what the strictly orthodox might think disrespectful ways. Again and again he inserted in his letters from Nevada the characteristic words and modes of expression of the King James Version: "You wish to know where I am, and where I have been? And, verily, you shall be satisfied. Behold, I am in the middle of the universe—at the centre of gravitation—even Carson City. And I have been to the land that floweth with gold and silver—Humboldt."[18] When he became a reporter, first for the Virginia City *Territorial Enterprise* and later for other western papers, he continued to put his knowledge of the Bible to good use. He seems to have had two purposes in so doing: humor and criticism. As in his letters home, he often achieved humor by inserting biblical expressions in accounts of contemporary events. Reporting a convention, for example, he related that the Hon. John K. Lovejoy "made honorable mention of the Legislature and the Committee on Internal Improvements. He told how the fountains of their great deep were broken up, and they rained forty days and forty nights, and brought on a flood of toll roads over the whole land."[19]

His feuds with rival reporters were often sparked by biblical humor. One such rival was a reporter for the Virginia City *Daily Union*, Clement T. Rice, whom he had dubbed "the Unreliable." In an *Enterprise* letter,

Clemens, who was now signing himself Mark Twain, let fly at Rice's eating abilities: "I am of the opinion that none of his ancestors were present when the five thousand were miraculously fed in the old Scriptural times. I base my opinion upon the twelve baskets of scraps and the little fishes that remained over after that feast. If the Unreliable himself had been there, the provisions would just about have held out, I think."[20] In California, where his opponent was "Fitz Smythe" (Albert S. Evans), Twain concocted a piece called "Remarkable Dream," in which he tells of dreaming that he was visited by the celebrated liars of Acts 5, Ananias and Sapphira, who dub Fitz Smythe a "knight of the Grand Order of the Liars of St. Ananias."[21] The narrator of the story is rather casual in his treatment of Ananias, remarking, "Yes, yes, yes, I remember you made a little statement that wouldn't wash, so to speak, and they took your life for it. They—they bounced a thunderbolt on your head, or something of that sort, didn't they?"[22] Here Twain was reversing his earlier formula: instead of biblical language applied to a modern situation, he now produced modern slang to depict a biblical scene.

Still more audacious humor appears in Twain's mock rhapsodizing over Obookia, a Sandwich Island native who had been converted to Christianity. Visiting the islands as correspondent for a California newspaper, he muses: "Here that gentle spirit worshipped ... on this altar, possibly, he broiled his venerable grandfather, and presented the rare offering before the high priest, who may have said, 'Well done, good and faithful servant.' It filled me with emotion."[23] The connecting of the phrase from the parable of the talents with the cooking of human flesh apparently struck Twain as genuinely humorous and was used by him on at least two other occasions, most notably as a proposed epitaph for a Negro cook who had been burned to death.[24] Twain could, incidentally, use the phrase in a completely serious context, as in his unusual but apparently sincere praise of the missionaries to the Sandwich Islands: "You may well say, 'Well done, good and faithful servants!' for mortal man could not have accomplished more with such material to work upon."[25]

In using the Bible as a source of humor, Twain was in the tradition of western writers such as his colleague Dan De Quille (William Wright).[26] Artemus Ward (Charles Farrar Browne), one of the most celebrated humorists of the day, whom Twain met in Nevada, was known for his solemn look and habit of slipping biblical words and phrases into his conversation.[27] Twain got some of his humorous effects in precisely that way, but though he may have been confirmed in the practice by his meeting with Ward, he had been doing it previously. Twain's use of the Bible did not, however, stop with employing its humorous possibilities.

He exposed the mercenary-mindedness and hypocrisy of the clergy to ridicule in a series of letters which he called "Important Correspondence between Mr. Mark Twain of San Francisco, and Rev. Bishop Hawks, D.D., of New York ... Concerning the Occupancy of Grace Cathedral." The bishop, talking of certain financial arrangements, writes: "I closed with them on these terms, my dear Mark, for I feel that so long as not even the little sparrows are suffered to fall to the ground unnoted, I shall be mercifully cared for; and besides, I know that come what may, I can always eke out an existence so long as the cotton trade holds out as good as it is now."[28] The good bishop is of course being gently criticized for his undue concern with the financial aspects of life. As Twain remarks, he "is not going to take his chances altogether with ... the little sparrows that are subject to accidents." But perhaps we should say that it is not the Bishop's concern with money that irks Twain so much as his pretense in the last passage quoted that he believes God will take care of him. In fact, it is here that we see emerging what is to be a major theme with Twain, his attack on hypocrisy and sham. In Twain's opinion a major object of pretense was the Bible. People claimed to revere it and to take its statements seriously, but they were for the most part like Bishop Hawks: talking of the little sparrows, they really had in mind the cotton trade.

Matthew 10:29 ("Are not two sparrows sold for a farthing? and one of them shall not fall on the ground without your Father") seems always to have struck Twain as a shallow passage; whenever a character of his uses it, he can safely be set down as either a hypocrite or a pious fool. Twice he included the expression in pretended newspaper accounts,[29] thus indicating what seemed to him the way in which the official culture keeps up its pretenses of being religious. In one of his later writings Twain vented his irritation with those who quote the verse unthinkingly: when Ursula, in "The Mysterious Stranger," declares that "Not a sparrow falls to the ground without His seeing it," Little Satan replies, "But it falls just the same. What good is seeing it fall?"[30]

Increasingly Mark Twain's works came to illustrate the kind of opposition Henry Nash Smith labels dominant culture versus vernacular protest.[31] In the story "The Scriptural Panoramist," for instance, the voice of the panorama exhibitor is that of the dominant culture, full of the expected pieties. His pianist, however, pro-

ceeds to puncture the mood by singularly inappropri-
ate accompanying music. The panorama of Christ's
calming the waters of Galilee is accompanied by "A
Life on the Ocean Wave" and that of his raising Lazarus from the dead by the lines: "Come rise up, William Ri-i-ley, And go along with me!" (*Writings*,
XIX, 392–93). The irreverence is attributed to someone other than Mark Twain; he was not yet ready to
speak for himself in that manner. The same holds true
for the Sandwich Island letters of 1866 and for some
of the letters from Europe and the Holy Land written
in the following year. In them a fictitious traveling
companion named Brown takes the position really held
by Twain while the latter is left to voice that of the
dominant society. When Brown observes that the is-
landers are carrying too far their mourning for a dead
princess, Twain counters by citing the example of
Jesus in a style which parodies the pious manner of
certain Bible quoters: "did not he mourn for the dead
Lazarus? Do not the sacred scriptures say 'Jesus
wept'?" Brown mutters "something about the imitation
being rather overdone or improved on," and as the fu-
neral rites continue he is heard again saying, "Jesus
wept," with the emphasis obviously on the second
word. Twain rebuked him but acknowledged that "the
gentle grief of the Savior was but poorly imitated
here."[32] Ministers who methodically used the Bible as
padding for their books also came under Brown's fire:
"when there is a chapter to be filled out, and they
haven't got anything to fill it out with, they shovel in
a lot of Scripture—now *don't* they? ... and when
they come to the volcano, or any sort of heavy scenery, and it is too much bother to describe it, they
shovel in another lot of Scripture, and wind up with
'Lo! what God hath wrought!' Confound their lazy

melts! Now, *I* wouldn't make extracts out of no such bosh" (*Letters from Hawaii*, 211). That Twain was impatient with some Bible quoters in his own family at this time is shown by his letter from Honolulu to Orion Clemens's wife concerning his bungling a chance to sell their Tennessee land: "It is no use to quote Scripture to me, Mollie,—I am in poverty & exile now because of Orion's religious scruples."[33]

In one of Twain's newspaper letters prior to his sailing for Europe on the *Quaker City* he describes a visit to Bible House in New York City, the printing establishment of the American Bible Society.[34] For three hours he wandered through the building, enjoying it more than a circus—such was his comparison—and giving further evidence of the truth of what he had written in 1864: "although I am not a very dusty Christian myself, I take an absorbing interest in religious affairs" (*Letters*, I, 96). Twain was interested in the many different kinds of Bibles in various languages. Of an Arabic Bible he wrote, "it fascinated me rather more than the old regular Bible I am accustomed to does. . . . It was a sort of a fresh, new sensation to see the last end of the good book, because I hadn't been there before for some time" (*Travels with Mr. Brown*, 204–205). Although this may have been part of Twain's "bad boy" pose, it does not seem likely that he did much Bible reading between his departure from Hannibal in 1853 and his approaching the Holy Land in 1867.

Twain bestowed high praise on Bible House, calling it "one of the chief among the fountain-heads of civilization in this great city, (if not *the* chief,)" (202). Almost like an evangelist, he asked: "why need men be ignorant of the Word? The great city of New York has within her limits no institution she has more reason to be proud of than this colossal Bible Association" (209). Such words sound strange indeed in view of Twain's diatribes against missionaries, for of course one of the chief tasks of Bible House was to supply Bibles for the mission field. But he ends by puncturing the solemn tone: "I believe I am done. I haven't had such a moral siege for a year. I will now go out and black-guard somebody till I begin to feel natural again" (213).

The seriousness of the essay is further broken by Twain's use of a new device, pretended ignorance about the Bible in order to get a laugh from the reader, who can congratulate himself on not being quite so stupid as Twain: "On this counter are laid piles of folded chapters of the Bible, side by side—piles of the Books of Esau, Isaac and Jacob, Matthew, Mark and Genesis, Chapter 1, 2, 3, and so on, each chapter to itself—and that woman shins around inside of that counter and snakes off a chapter from each pile as fast as a printer picks up types, and before you could ask her out to drink she has stacked up a complete Bible straight through from Exodus to Deuteronomy!"[35]

The Bible House report effectively illustrates the two sides of Twain's nature which were apparent by now, one inherited from Hannibal fundamentalism and the other from John Marshall Clemens, John Quarles, Thomas Paine, and Freemasonry. There was the side completely acceptable to the dominant culture, the "good people" of society, that could hail Bible House as "one of the chief among the fountain-heads of civilization," and there was the other side, representing a minority protest, which could introduce slang and the idea of going out for a drink into a picture made to order for pious and sentimental persons, that of a dedicated woman assembling Bibles to be used in the conversion and Christian nurture of the heathen peoples of some far-off land. In the Sandwich Island letters such an irreverent thought would probably have come from Brown, but Twain was now undertaking the irreverence himself. It is for this reason that, although he appears at first, Brown soon disappears from the *Quaker City* letters and is absent altogether from *The Innocents Abroad:* Twain had taken over his role. But the Twain who had been Brown's opposite, with his phrases about "the sacred scriptures," was not completely gone. For all his hatred of pretended piety and solemn tones, Twain could use them occasionally. He had within him something of both the Scriptural Panoramist and his pianist, of both "Twain" and Brown. Desiring to criticize society, he also wished its approval. The impulses to piety and reverence came to the surface and had their day later. But the next event to be considered is the *Quaker City* excursion where irreverence was for Twain the key word.

2.

To The Holy Land

O**N** **JUNE** 8, 1867, the steamship *Quaker City* sailed from New York on what was perhaps the first pleasure excursion by American tourists to Europe and the Holy Land. Although the passenger list was originally to have included such men as Henry Ward Beecher and William Tecumseh Sherman, Mark Twain found himself the closest thing to a real celebrity on board. Thirty-one years old, chiefly known as a lecturer and author of "Jim Smiley and His Jumping Frog," he had been hired as newspaper correspondent for the San Francisco *Alta California* and the New York *Tribune* and assigned to send back periodic reports of what he later called "The New Pilgrim's Progress." Few of his writings—other than those specifically biblical, such as *Letters from the Earth*—draw on the Bible so much as these reports and the book he developed out of them, *The Innocents Abroad.*

Little time was required for Twain to discover that his fellow passengers were not his notion of ideal companions. Many of them were advanced in age, and almost all of them seemed disgustingly pious. The irreverent westerner soon gathered around him a group of cronies—including his future brother-in-law—and had little connection with the respectable majority group, except for Mary Mason Fairbanks, wife of the publisher of the Cleveland *Herald*, who so took him under her wing that she called her "Mother" for the rest of her life. Undoubtedly the piety exhibited by the more orthodox participants heightened Twain's irreverence. "There was a little difference between us—nothing more," he observed at the tour's end. "They thought they could have saved Sodom and Gomorrah, and I thought it would have been unwise to risk money on it."[1]

Twain biographers customarily note that while at Constantinople he bought a Bible and began studying it diligently, so as to be prepared for travel in the Holy Land. This fact may be partly misleading, for Twain was making use of the Bible in pre-Constantinople letters, and at least one of them clearly shows that he had access to a Bible—probably one in the ship's library.[2] It is true, of course, that when he finally arrived in the Holy Land, Twain's newspaper reports began to fill up with Bible characters, stories, and geography, and to be liberally sprinkled with biblical quotations. He seems to have visited and written up almost every biblical locale, from the place where Balaam's ass lived ("holy ground," he said)[3] to the site of the crucifixion.

But while the other "pilgrims" were being impressed and awed by all they saw, in the manner of the authors of the Holy Land guidebooks they had read, Twain became thoroughly disillusioned and confessed it: "Thus, one by one, the splendid attractions of Palestine are passing away—gradually, but surely, the paint and the gilding are peeling from its cheap theatrical scenery and exposing the unsightly boards beneath"

(*Traveling*, 254). A false impression is given by some writers who have attempted to describe what Twain wrote about the Holy Land. Albert Bigelow Paine, his official biographer, remarks that "the Syrian chapters in *The Innocents Abroad* are permeated with the poetry and legendary beauty of the Bible story" (*Biography*, 338). Van Wyck Brooks goes further astray when he tells us that Twain's "attention had been fixed in his childhood upon the civilization of the biblical lands, and that is why they seemed to him so full of poetry and dignity." Because of "the initiation of the Sunday school" Twain is said to have been reverent in the Holy Land.[4] How such a verdict could be passed, in view of what Twain really said in *The Innocents Abroad*, and especially in the *Alta* letters, is hard to imagine.

The very cornerstone of Twain's treatment of the Holy Land was irreverence: he told slangy versions of Bible stories, rechristened Palestinian towns with American names (Caesarea Philippi became Baldwinsville), referred familiarly to venerable patriarchs as "old Moses" and "old Adam," called Nimrod a "brick," had the angels "flitting" up and down Jacob's ladder, parodied biblical style, and reached the height of disregard for propriety in a fleering lament: "Poor Lot's wife is gone—I never think of her without feeling sad. The cattle must have got her. There is something infinitely touching in the thought. Hers was too sad a history to jest about. I might speak with levity of Lot himself, or of Goliah, or many other of the Patriarchs, but whenever I think of poor Lot's wife I feel no longer in a mood for flippant speeches. Peace to her sediment!"[5] As a matter of fact, Twain's view is as little like that of the Hannibal Sunday school, or of the dominant society in general, as possible, and this is nowhere more evident than in his retelling of the Genesis story of Joseph.

In *The Innocents Abroad* the Joseph story is introduced as one of the beautiful passages "in a book ... gemmed with beautiful passages,"[6] but in his letter for the *Alta California* Twain mercilessly ridiculed and criticized both story and style. Biblical style, slang, legitimate paraphrase, and quotations from elsewhere in the Bible were fused with deliberate alterations of the original story. Joseph, as the *Alta* narrator tells it, "used to swell around and put on many frills among his brethren." Trouble soon arose, "for, behold, even before these days were they down upon him." When one brother urges that Joseph be pitied, Twain continues: "Wherefore they pitted him. And the self-same pit that they pitted him in is here in this place, even to this day." The sale of Joseph to the Ishmaelites went "at the ruling rates, ten per cent off for cash."[7]

The tale of Potiphar's wife received from Twain a new interpretation. Genesis makes it clear that Joseph is blameless, but Twain has it that Joseph "got into trouble with Potiphar's wife at last, and both gave in their versions of the affair, but the lady's was plausible and Joseph's was most outrageously shaky" (*Traveling*, 222). Restored to favor, Joseph "had the run of the whole establishment," and there followed a remarkable conversation in which Joseph said to Pharaoh: " 'Behold, thou and thy servant can gather together divers and sundry shekels out of this thing—let us bear the market and buy against the season of famine.' And Pharoah said, 'I perceive that thou art not of them that know not to come in when it doth rain; behold, it shall be even as thou sayest.' "[8] In a phrase based on one in Revelation, Twain continued: "Before a time and a half or two times had passed over their heads, Joseph and Pharaoh owned about two-thirds of Egypt."[9]

Twain deliberately twisted his story at the point where Benjamin and his brothers depart from the palace, having received the desired food to sustain them in the famine. Genesis records that Joseph ordered his steward to put his silver cup into the mouth of Benjamin's sack, but Twain wrote that Benjamin "with the artless simplicity of youth, nipped a silver cup."[10] When it is discovered that Benjamin has the presumably stolen cup, there is "weeping and wailing and gnashing of teeth," a combination of expressions appearing in Matthew and Luke.[11] The reunion scene between Joseph and Benjamin became in Twain's account a satirical hit at the "recognition scene" of sentimental drama: Joseph "fell upon Benjamin's neck and cried: 'Ha! the strawberry upon your left arm!—it is! it is my long-lost brother!' (slow music.)"[12]

When Jacob, the father of Joseph, Benjamin, and the other ten brothers, receives the good news that his son is alive, Twain employs a sentence closely modeled on a recurring formula in Kings and in Chronicles: "The joy of Jacob, and the words that he spake, are they not written in the chronicles of the book that is called Genesis?"[13] Then comes another reunion scene over which pious Bible readers had long shed tears, but Twain swept away all sentimentality: "So Jacob went down into the land of Egypt, and tripped and fell upon Joseph's neck; but Joseph caught him all right, and said 'Go slow, Governor.'"[14] After this wild romp through Scripture, the ending of the story in the *Alta* letter contradicts all that has preceded it, striking precisely the same note one finds at the beginning of the story in *Innocents Abroad:* "So ends the story of Joseph—the most touching and beautiful, and also the most dramatic, in the Old Testament. Of all the patriarchs, Joseph was the noblest. In his perfect character, one can find no flaw."[15]

In *Innocents Abroad* Twain told Joseph's story in conventional language and diminished his reputation only by suggesting that perhaps Esau—usually dismissed as an unimportant and rather stupid fellow who sold his birthright for a mess of pottage—was greater than Joseph. The suggestion was a startling one, especially so because it appeared in the book, generally more conservative than the newspaper letters. The gist of Twain's argument appears in his conclusion: "Who stands first—outcast Esau forgiving Jacob in prosperity, or Joseph on a King's throne forgiving the ragged tremblers whose happy rascality had placed him there?"[16] Here was a fresh insight, the result of reading the Bible with one's own eyes rather than with those of Bible commentaries, ministers, and Sunday school teachers.

By contrast, one of the few biblical stories Twain managed to tell with some seriousness is that of the conversion of Paul. To be too casual about Paul would of course have been riskier than what Twain had done with Joseph. But at least one notable pleasantry creeps in concerning "the street called Straight" into which Ananias was commanded to go in order to find Paul: "The street called Straight is straighter than a corkscrew, but not as straight as a rainbow. St. Luke is careful not to commit himself; he does not say it is the street which is straight, but 'the street which is *called* Straight.' It is a fine piece of irony; it is the only facetious remark in the Bible, I believe. St. Luke probably considered it the best thing he ever said."[17]

Besides Twain's critical and freewheeling attitude toward the Bible stories there were instances in which he expressly doubted the truth of the Bible's historical statements. For one thing, he thought the Bible vastly overestimated the number of inhabitants which the land had. Discussing one of Joshua's "exterminating battles," he quotes Judges 11:4: "And they went out, they and all their hosts with them, much people, even as the sand that is upon the sea shore for multitude." Parenthetically he added a sentence which does not appear in *Innocents Abroad:* "There were probably about ten thousand—there is hardly country enough in all the land around here to support more."[18] More pointedly, Twain observed in a later letter that if Nevada could support the entire population of the United States then one might believe that Palestine could have supported the six million supposedly there in Bible times. And then he added: "it don't look promising to me. The land must have been blessed much harder then than ever it was cursed afterwards."[19] Twain definitely thought the Bible unrealistic in its praise of the land. In this connection he cited the report of the spies concerning the area around Dan: "We have seen the land, and behold it is very good. ... A place where there is no want of anything that is in the earth."[20] Said Twain: "They drew it just a little strong when they said it was 'a place where there is no want of anything. ...' That was a *little* strong."[21] To his notebook Twain confided: "The ravens could hardly make their own living, let alone board Elijah."[22]

Again and again Twain expressed distaste for the land and its people. And now he became equally disgusted with the Bible, as he realized that the persons before him must be much like those so venerated in the Sunday schools and by pious Bible readers: "When I see these hooded, full-robed, bearded, swarthy Arabs riding on a mighty-eared jackass the size of a young calf, and swinging their prodigious feet contentedly to and fro within four inches of the ground, and pouring forth that maddening caterwauling which they call music, my heart goes back to the old days of the patriarchs and I behold the pride of Canaan and the hope of the world—Israel the blest!" (*Traveling*, 217). The Good Samaritan, he opined, "was probably the only good Samaritan the province ever produced" (*Traveling*, 258). His revulsion extended even to the royalty of the Bible: "I cannot be imposed upon any more by that picture of the Queen of Sheba visiting Solomon. I shall say to myself, You look fine, madam, but your feet are not clean, and you smell like a camel" (*Writings*, II, 310).

By this time one may well wish to ask, Was Twain reverent in any way in his letters from the Holy Land? Yes, he was. At least one biblical passage had a special appeal for him: " 'Like unto the shadow of a great rock in a weary land.' Nothing in the Bible is more beautiful than that, and surely there is no place we have wandered to that is able to give it such touching expression as this blistering, naked, treeless land."[23]

At times during his Holy Land journey Twain appealed to the Bible for argumentative support, just as any orthodox Christian might do. When some members of the party suggested that they should ride their horses extra hard so as to reach Damascus in two days instead of three, thus avoiding travel on the Sabbath, Twain's ire was aroused: "We said the Saviour, who pitied dumb beasts and taught that the ox must be rescued from the mire even on the Sabbath day, would not have counseled a forced march like this ... they were willing to commit a sin against the spirit of religious law, in order that they might preserve the letter of it. It was not worth while to tell them 'the letter

kills.' "[24] Ironically, Twain was using the Bible to re-
buke those who were most ready to proclaim their al-
legiance to it, and he was surely delighted that his fellow "sinners" should be more Christian than the self-
righteous "pilgrims."

Above all, Twain was reverent in dealing with
Christ. As in the passage just quoted, he almost always
refers to him in an orthodox manner, usually as "the
Saviour," "the Lord," "Christ," or by one of his titles,
such as "the Prince of Peace." In recounting the events
of Jesus's life, Twain was never flippant or mocking;
the language is straightforward and devoid of slang
and humorous sallies against the characteristics of the
King James Version. And, although he told his readers
that most of the biblical sites he visited were "imag-
inary holy places created by the monks," at the traditional place of the crucifixion he declared that one
"fully believes that he is looking upon the place where
the Saviour gave up his life."[25] The only note of levity
in connection with Christ comes when he jokes about
the Second Coming, saying it will never take place in
Palestine; no sensible man who had been there once
would want to come again. First recorded in Twain's
notebook, the remark appears in an *Alta* letter attributed to "a grave gentleman."[26] Twain realized that
he was being a little daring and, as he had with Brown,
shifted at least part of the responsibility to someone
else.

It should also be said that Twain's use of the Bible
in connection with the Holy Land excursion was not
wholly serious or sardonically humorous. There certainly are moments of lighter biblical humor, the most
famous being his conduct at the tomb of Adam. To
the readers of the *Alta* he reported how he "shed some
tender tears over poor old Adam," who had died so

young that he had not seen the telegraph, the locomotive, the steamboat, or even the flood (*Traveling*, 273). In *Innocents Abroad* Twain retained the tears and dwelt upon Adam's being "a blood relation." "Noble old man," he mused, "he did not live to see me. ... And I—I—alas, I did not live to see *him*. ... Let us trust that he is better off where he is. Let us take comfort in the thought that his loss is our eternal gain" (*Writings*, II, 338).

In September the Holy Land journey ended. The *Quaker City* visited a few other countries, notably Egypt and Spain, and returned to New York in the middle of November 1867. Said Twain in a letter to the New York *Herald:* "If ever those children of Israel in Palestine forget when Gideon's band went through there from America they ought to be cursed once more and finished."[27]

Several points about Twain and the Bible stand out as one looks back at the *Quaker City* letters: his considerable knowledge of the Bible, his versatility in using it, and his skeptical irreverence as contrasted with the extravagant piety of the majority of the passengers. No orthodox believer when he left New York, he found that closer knowledge of the Bible and its land made him a still greater skeptic. The frequently irreverent letters sent back to San Francisco and New York must have seemed quite shocking to many readers, especially in their offhand attitude toward such standard heroes as Joseph. It is little wonder that a minister in the former city should refer to "This son of the Devil, Mark Twain!"[28] And yet, Twain could have gone much further. He made no criticism of the biblical concept of God; he had nothing critical to say about Jesus. He never openly challenged the authority of the Bible on an important matter. Perhaps there was some truth in his rather surprising statement that he had been "taught to revere the Scriptures, and that reverence is pretty firmly grounded" (*Traveling*, 166). Twain's criticism of the Bible reached in the *Quaker City* letters a higher level than ever before, but after an intervening period of reversal, it was to rise to far greater heights, culminating in such works as *Letters from the Earth*, left unpublished until 1962, and certain autobiographical dictations of 1906, which did not appear until 1963.

What Twain had to say about the Bible in these letters from abroad is not unlike what he says of almost everything that comes under his scrutiny in Europe and the Holy Land: it does not deserve its reputation. Again and again he made the point that what he saw fell short of descriptions he had read or pictures he had seen. Paris barber shops, the Louvre and the "old masters" in general, the Arno river, Turkish baths, the Sea of Galilee—all come under the same condemnation. Phrases such as "another romantic fraud" and "shameless humbug" are scattered throughout his letters. Twain believed that literature too could be a romantic fraud, and meted out to the story of Abelard and Heloise much the same flippant treatment he had given the story of Joseph. Nor could the incipient realist resist a swipe at Fenimore Cooper's noble Indians as "an extinct tribe which never existed" (*Writings*, I, 264). Although Twain admittedly encountered some sights in Europe that he admired very much (Versailles, the cathedral of Milan), the dominant impression one receives from reading *Innocents Abroad* and the travel letters which preceded it is of a catalog of fakes and frauds which have received both too much veneration and too many tears.

This misplaced adoration would not have existed,

25

Twain believed, if people had been honest about what they saw. His fellow pilgrims irritated him by their inability to see anything other than what they believed they ought to see. As he tells it, even the phrasing of their admiring comments was "smouched" from the gushing guidebooks they were reading. They were apparently afraid to trust their own vision and admit what they were really seeing. "The pilgrims will tell of Palestine, when they get home," Twain wrote, "not as it appeared to *them*, but as it appeared to Thompson and Robinson and Grimes—with the tints varied to suit each pilgrim's creed" (*Writings*, II, 272). They were guilty of the sin Thomas Paine termed "mental lying." But Twain made it clear that his companions were only following the lead of others who had described the Holy Land in terms of what they wanted to see rather than what was really before their eyes. Such illusion might take two forms: it might simply describe some feature of the land in glowing terms, ignoring its bad aspects; or it might introduce theological bias: "I am sure, from the tenor of books I have read, that many who have visited this land in years gone by, were Presbyterians, and came seeking evidences in support of their particular creed; they found a Presbyterian Palestine, and they had already made up their minds to find no other, though possibly they did not know it, being blinded by their zeal. Others were Baptists, seeking Baptist evidences and a Baptist Palestine. Others were Catholics, Methodists, Episcopalians, seeking evidences indorsing their several creeds. ... Honest as these men's intentions may have been, they were full of partialities and prejudices, they entered the country with their verdicts already prepared, and they could no more write dispassionately and impartially about it than they could about their own wives and children"

(*Writings*, II, 270–71). Although it may be objected that Twain found a skeptic's Palestine, he was trying hard to tell the real truth about the lands he visited and the famous sights he saw, independent of and unhampered by the reports of previous visitors. In his preface, written in San Francisco some months after the excursion ended, he stated that his purpose was "to suggest to the reader how *he* would be likely to see Europe and the East if he looked at them with his own eyes instead of the eyes of those who travelled in those countries before him." "I make small pretense," he continued, "of showing any one how he *ought* to look at objects of interest beyond the sea—other books do that" (*Writings*, I, xxxvii). Twain wanted to report what he as an individual saw, whether it be in a European art museum, in the Church of the Holy Sepulchre in Jerusalem, or in the pages of the Bible itself. Consequently, Twain tried to tell the truth about the Bible too, though he softened much of his criticism before publishing *Innocents Abroad*. He believed that with the Bible no less than with the hallowed shrines of Europe and the Holy Land, people were filled with sentimentality and credulity about its contents and found objective treatment difficult. Baptists, Catholics, and the rest open its covers just as they enter Palestine—seeking confirmation of what they already believe. Twain's view of the Bible in 1867 appears to be much like what he is saying throughout *Innocents Abroad* and the letters on which it is based: there is good here, but there is also a great deal which is not half so fine as the romantic sentimentalists and special pleaders would have us believe. For in a sense these letters are Twain's declaration of independence, not merely from Europe but from all subservience to accepted, time-honored points of view. They are his proclamation that he is an individual, unhampered by group control, free to pass his own judgments. He may not have been as free as he thought he was, either from convention or from sentimentality. Nevertheless, he was trying to stand for sincerity and individualism. If he was irreverent in the process, one can only offer in justification his own statement: "Irreverence is the champion of liberty and its only sure defense" (*Notebook*, 195).

3.

Three Biblical Images

Fictional parallels to biblical characters frequently recur in Twain's writings. Occasionally the characters themselves point out the resemblance, as when the Connecticut Yankee compares his rise in the kingdom with that of Joseph (*Writings*, XVI, 64). Twain scholars have recognized several less explicit parallels. Paschal Covici, for example, analyzes the "Legend of the Spectacular Ruin" in *A Tramp Abroad*, showing its relationship to the story of Christ and to that of David and Goliath.[1] Albert E. Stone finds two parallels with the story of Christ: in *The Prince and the Pauper*, Tom Canty spurns his mother with words suggesting Peter's denial,[2] and in its sacrificial nature, the death of Joan of Arc resembles Christ's death.[3] In the mock account of his ascent of the Riffleberg in *A Tramp Abroad*, Twain is like Moses leading the Israelites through the wilderness (*Writings*, IV, 113). And in *Tom Sawyer, Detective* occurs a scene reminiscent of God's questioning Cain as to the whereabouts of Abel. A Negro comes in to tell Uncle Silas Phelps that Brace Dunlap wants his brother and that Uncle Silas should tell him where he is. At once Uncle Silas replies, "Am

I his brother's keeper?" Later we learn that Uncle Silas erroneously believes that he has killed the brother being inquired for, thus strengthening the parallel suggested by the variation on Cain's "Am I my brother's keeper?"[4]

What Twain did with the Bible stories just mentioned was of little significance compared with his far more extensive use of three major biblical images: the Prodigal Son; Adam, Eve, and the fall; Noah and the flood. The biblical characters Twain mentioned more than any other were Adam, Christ, Noah, and the Prodigal Son.[5] Genesis is mentioned far more than any other book, and Luke, in which the story of the Prodigal Son is told, is used more than any other New Testament book except Matthew.[6]

Superficial reasons for Twain's attraction to these three stories may readily be found. In the first place, they were among the best known parts of the Bible, both for Twain and for his audience. If one knows anything about the Old Testament, he is likely to know the stories of the first eleven chapters of Genesis (including those of Adam and Noah) and those of the four Gospels (including such parables of Jesus as the Prodigal Son). Since so many of Twain's references are drawn from the first eleven chapters of Genesis, it seems clear that he was fascinated by the beginnings of things. No doubt his deterministic philosophy was partly responsible for this; in "The Turning Point of My Life," published in 1910, he asserted that at the beginning events occurred which inexorably shaped the present. Adam was a symbol—though many took him for a historical figure—of the beginning of the human race, while Noah represented a new beginning. The Prodigal Son story also tells of a man who made a new beginning, though on a far lesser scale. Finally it must be noted that as an old riverboatman Twain would naturally be drawn to the biblical story in which water and a ship figure most prominently.

But there were deeper reasons for his attraction to these characters, chiefly the resemblances which Twain saw between them and himself. A figure that interested Twain greatly was the exile from Paradise—the man who once knew joy and happiness and lived in an ideal world but who now finds himself in an evil one, far removed from the old. Twain found in the Bible two men like this: the Prodigal Son and Adam. The difference between the two was that the Prodigal was able to return home and to know once more the joy that had been his; Adam was banished from Eden forever. As we shall see, there were moments in the period 1867–1870 when Twain saw himself as a returning prodigal. But after 1870, and especially in the fifteen years before his death, he saw himself not as the Prodigal but rather as another Adam exiled from Paradise. In Adam's life as in his own, Twain thought the beginning the best part of all. It is surely no coincidence that most of his best works—*Huckleberry Finn, Tom Sawyer, Life on the Mississippi*—drew on his recollections of an earlier and better time. As he saw it, few things live up to their early promise. Noah, too, left behind the world that he had known, though with less reluctance than Adam, after having warned his neighbors of the coming destruction which their folly was to bring. In his later years Twain came also to identify himself with Noah, regarding his own civilization as under a similar threat.

THE PRODIGAL SON story was used most conspicuously in the years immediately following Twain's return from Europe and the Holy Land. In the fifteenth chapter of the gospel of Luke we are told how the Pharisees and scribes murmured against Jesus because of his receiving and eating with sinners. To justify his conduct, Jesus relates a series of parables, including that of the Prodigal Son (verses 11–32). The story is of a father and his two sons. The younger receives his inheritance, leaves home, wastes his money "with riotous living," despairs in the low situation to which he is brought, returns home, and is joyfully received by his father. A feast is held, at which the principal meat is the "fatted calf"; the older brother now strenuously objects to what he regards as the father's unfair conduct. The father protests his love for the older son but urges the rightness of his action: "It was meet that we should make merry, and be glad: for this thy brother was dead, and is alive again; and was lost, and is found." The point is similar to that of another parable related in the same chapter: "joy shall be in heaven over one sinner, that repenteth, more than over ninety and nine just persons, which need no repentance."

Twain's earliest use of the passage is in the story of "The Scriptural Panoramist," where the pious voice of the panoramist describes a picture of the Prodigal's return: "Observe the happy expression just breaking over the features of the poor, suffering youth—so worn and weary with his long march; note also the ecstasy beaming from the uplifted countenance of the aged father, and the joy that sparkles in the eyes of the excited group of youths and maidens and seems ready to burst into the welcoming chorus from their lips. The lesson, my friends, is as solemn and instructive as the story is tender and beautiful." The mood is shattered as the pianist plays: "Oh, we'll all get blind drunk, / When Johnny comes marching home!" (*Writings*, XIX, 392–93).

Twain provides his own irreverence without bothering to attribute it to someone else when he retells the story in a letter to the *Alta California* dated "Nazareth, September, 1867." Talking of the village of Deburich, he declares it is "full of interest" because the Prodigal Son was "born and raised here." Introducing the story as "touching and suggestive," Twain proceeds to a mocking description of the Prodigal's home: "In the mansion was there nothing lacking; there was a bowl and a spoon, and also a calabash. Yet were not these people proud ... every seventh day he ate of the broth of goat's meat and the luscious milk of asses. He lacked not anything that human heart could wish" (*Traveling*, 246). Mixing current slang and biblical language, Twain declares that "Elsewhere, in all the coasts of Galilee, was not another swell like unto him." Though he uses some pseudobiblical language ("wherefore," "in the fulness of time"), he also employs genuine phrases from the biblical account ("a far country," "riotous living," "I will arise and go to my father," "fell on his neck and kissed him"). Twain's account follows Luke fairly well, though he reports one scene having no biblical basis at all: "Then went he to the Publican that erst had welcomed him with joy and gladness, and said, Behold, thy servant is naked and hungry, and penniless, and like to die with thirst; open thy gates, I pray thee. But the Publican laughed him to scorn, and said, Get thee to honest labor—put shekels in thy purse."[7] In concluding, Twain recalls his boyhood notion of the Prodigal as "the stupidest youth that ever lived" and of his home as a "palace where he had a dozen courses for dinner, and wore handsome clothes, and had fast horses, and dogs, and plenty of money to spend" and stresses the contrast with his present conception: "But my dream is over, now. It was just about an even matter between the Prodigal's two homes. If he had had a shirt and something to eat when he was feeding swine, the difference between that place and his old home would not have paid for the trouble of the journey back again—save that one was *home* and the other was not" (*Traveling*, 248). None of this Prodigal Son story found its way into *Innocents Abroad.*

The story of the Prodigal came to have a good deal more meaning for Twain as he found himself playing that role, with the part of the father being taken by two members of the opposite sex: Mary Mason Fairbanks, whom he had met on the *Quaker City* excursion, and Olivia ("Livy") Langdon, whose brother Charles had also been a passenger and was the means of bringing the two together. Mrs. Fairbanks had taken Twain and some of the other young men on the *Quaker City* under her wing in such a way that all were shortly calling her "Mother." Twain wrote his family that "she sewed my buttons on, kept my clothes in presentable trim, fed me on Egyptian jam, (when I behaved,) lectured me awfully on the quarterdeck on moonlit promenading evenings, & cured me of several bad habits."[8] He was assuming the role of the reformed bad boy, a repentant prodigal who had seen the error of his ways. Something of the feeling which she inspired in him is suggested by his letter to a friend of hers at a time of great sorrow: "It is needless for me or for any one with only human lips to try to comfort her at a time like this—for words are vain & little worth, save those a true Christian such as she is knows where to seek. Come unto me all ye that labor & are heavy laden, & I will give you rest—*rest*. No words my lips might frame, could be so freighted with sympathy, so filled with peace. Even to me, sinner that I am, this is the most beautiful sentence that graces any page—the tenderest, the most touching, the softest to the ear. To her, then, standing in the light, it has a world of significance that I can only dimly imagine— not appreciate" (*Mrs. Fairbanks*, 11). Twain pictures himself as a "sinner," standing on the outside, but looking in and admiring what he sees. He admires the Bible too, and bestows high praise on a verse that in years to come would probably seem to him only bitter sarcasm.

Correspondence and visits went on between Twain and Mrs. Fairbanks from 1867 until shortly before her death in 1898, long after all resemblance between him and the Prodigal had ceased. The letters are, naturally enough, filled with biblical allusions. One scholar finds them "perhaps the most heavily Bible-saturated writings that Mark Twain ever did."[9] This may not be accurate, but certainly Twain drew heavily on the Bible as a book both he and Mrs. Fairbanks knew well. The longest and one of the most significant biblical passages is that in Twain's Christmas letter of 1868, written while he was working hard at the role of prodigal: "About this time . . . eighteen hundred & sixty nine years ago, the stars were shedding a purer lustre above the barren hills of Bethlehem—& possibly flowers were being charmed to life in the dismal plain where the Shepherds watched their flocks—& the hovering angels were singing Peace on earth, good-will to men. For the Saviour was come." He went on to ask Mrs. Fairbanks if she did not recall how Bethlehem looked and if the picture did not "mellow in the distance" and take on "the soft, unreal semblance" that poetry and tradition had given it: "Don't you realize again, as in other years, that Jesus *was* born there, & that the angels *did* sing in the still air above, & that the wondering shepherds *did* hold their breath & listen as the mysterious music floated by? *I* do. It is more real than ever. And I am glad, a hundred times glad, that I saw Bethlehem, though at the time it seemed that that sight had swept away forever, every pleasant fancy & every cherished memory that ever the City of Nativity had stored away in my mind & heart."[10]

Truly it seemed that the Prodigal had come home—home to America and home to orthodox piety, for this is plainly not the language of protest but of acceptance. And it was to Mrs. Fairbanks that he most often described himself as the Prodigal. He often signed his letters to her "Yr. Improving Prodigal" (*Mrs. Fairbanks*, 6), "The Reformed Prodigal" (24), "Your Returning Prodigal" (32), and once "The Prodigal in a far country chawing of husks ... & with nobody to molest or keep him straight. (!) mild exultation."[11] Advising Mrs. Fairbanks that he was coming to Cleveland, he urged her to "please stand ready to trot out your fatted calf."[12]

Twain obviously enjoyed sustaining the bad boy-good mother roles begun on board the *Quaker City*. But he was making a genuine effort—trying too hard, probably—to reform and become a Christian. In this he was aided by Mrs. Fairbanks but still more by another to whom he appeared as a prodigal, Olivia Langdon. The comparison was apparent to Twain; when he arrived at the Langdon home one morning in November 1868, before Livy had agreed to marry him, he announced to the family: "The calf has returned; may the prodigal have some breakfast?" (*Biography*, 375). At first Livy was reluctant to accept the suit of "the wild humorist of the Pacific slope," and it was with considerable perseverance that Twain held on through several rejections of his proposal. At last, however, he was successful. Livy accepted, and in biblical language he announced the glad fact to his friend the Rev. Joseph H. Twichell of Hartford: "Sound the loud timbrel!—and let yourself out to your most prodigious capacity—for I have fought the good fight and lo! I have won!"[13]

During his courtship of Livy, Twain became much like the Prodigal. Having strayed into the "far country" of religious skepticism, he now made a valiant effort to return to the orthodox religious faith which Livy held, and his letters are filled with expressions of this attempt. "Turn toward the Cross and be comforted," he wrote her in the year before they were married, "I turn with you—What would you more? The peace of God shall rest upon us, and all will be well" (*My Father*, 21). So reformed was he that in *Innocents Abroad* he was able to describe himself as "a humble and a consistent Christian" (*Writings*, I, 257). After the book's completion he went so far as to wish that there were not an irreverent passage in it (*Mrs. Fairbanks*, 110).

Naturally the Bible figured prominently in the letters which passed between Twain and Livy prior to their marriage. More than at any other time in his life, Twain spoke with great reverence for it. In a letter written early in 1869, he told her of the reading they would do when they married—Tennyson, Milton, Macaulay, Poe. "And," he continued, "out of the Book of Life you shall cull the wisdom that shall make our lives an anthem void of discord and our deeds a living worship of the God that gave them."[14] As would be proper for a budding Christian, a prodigal returning home, Twain was reading his Bible diligently and reporting to Livy: "Little dearie, little darling, in a few minutes, after I shall have read a Testament lesson & prayed for us both, as usual, I shall be in bed."[15] And in another letter he reports, "I have read VI Corinthians, Livy, & shall read more in the Bible before I go to bed" (*Mrs. Fairbanks*, 62). Dixon Wecter, editor of the love letters, states that some are "filled with scriptural texts" (*Mrs. Fairbanks*, 62). Livy was sending Twain material also; on one occasion he wrote her: "Thanks for the book, the sermon & the Bible notes" (*Mrs. Fairbanks*, 100).

Actually Twain's letters to Livy did not wholly display a returning prodigal's attitude in what they had to say about the Bible. Most did—one Christmas letter is much like that to Mrs. Fairbanks (*My Father*, 53)— but there is at least one which reveals that Twain had not cut himself off entirely from liberal thought: "I have been reading some new arguments to prove that the world is very old, & that the six days of creation were six immensely long periods. For instance, according to Genesis, the *stars* were made when the world was, yet this writer mentions the significant fact that there are stars within reach of our telescopes whose light requires 50,000 years to traverse the wastes of space & come to our earth" (*Love Letters*, 133). If Genesis were literally true, of course, no star could be more than six thousand years old, much less have existed 50,000 years ago to start light on its way to earth. Such reflections on astronomy were to lead Twain on to a theme which recurs with ever-increasing frequency in his later years: the insignificance of man and the dubiousness of the biblical view of him as "a little lower than the angels." Paraphrasing the verse from which that quotation comes, Twain asked, "Verily, What is Man, that he should be considered of God?"[16] Here, however, Twain presumably feels that man *is* considered of God and that it is truly remarkable that he is, considering his smallness in comparison to the vast universe. In time he would doubt that assumption.

The wedding took place at Livy's home town of Elmira, New York, on February 2, 1870.[17] Acting the part of returned Prodigal, of sinner turned Christian, Twain was agreeable that he and Livy should begin life together with Bible reading a part of the daily routine. Each morning they read a chapter together. To an old friend from the West, Joe Goodman, the sight of Twain saying grace at meals and joining in family worship was truly astounding (*Biography*, 411). But the Prodigal soon became restless. Those elements Goodman had known in Twain and the skepticism he had acquired over the years could not be permanently subdued. Before long Twain called a halt to the Bible readings, saying, according to Paine: "Livy, you may keep this up if you want to, but I must ask you to excuse me from it. It is making me a hypocrite. I don't believe in this Bible. It contradicts my reason. I can't sit here and listen to it, letting you believe that I regard it, as you do, in the light of gospel, the word of God."[18] He was himself heeding the plea for sincerity made in *Innocents Abroad*.

Although Twain did alter his *Quaker City* letters— and wished that he had further altered *Innocents Abroad*—and although he did have moments at which he felt he might become a Christian after all, moments in which the pious phrases of the dominant culture flowed freely, his basic attitudes toward the Bible remained unchanged. The biblical material found in most of his newspaper work during this time does not differ significantly from that written prior to the return of the *Quaker City*. To Mrs. Fairbanks and the Langdon family he had described himself as a returning prodigal and such he seemed for a time to be. But it was not long before he left the home of orthodoxy once more, never to return. His position was precisely that of the supposed writer of one of Tom Sawyer's "nonnamous letters": "I . . . have got religgion and wish to quit it and lead an honest life again."[19]

MARK TWAIN's interest in and his use of the Prodigal Son as an image for his own situation was now supplanted by images which had been in his mind for some time: Adam and Eve, the paradise of Eden, the pair's yielding to the temptations of Satan, and their expulsion from the garden. Adam had appeared in Twain's writings as far back as the 1852–1853 contributions to the Hannibal *Journal*, "Blabbing Government Secrets" and "Oh, She Has a Red Head," the latter signed "A Son of Adam."[20] Comparisons with Eden had occurred to him in Hawaii[21] and at Versailles.[22] The readers of *Innocents Abroad* had laughed over his tears shed at the supposed tomb of Adam in Jerusalem.[23] And in "Captain Stormfield's Visit to Heaven," begun in 1868, though not published until much later, he had pictured Adam as a great crowd-drawer in heaven, reporting that if he "was to show himself to every new comer that wants to call and gaze at him and strike him for his autograph, he would never had time to do anything but just that."[24]

If we can believe his account in *Is Shakespeare Dead?* (1909) interest in the fall of man goes all the way back to the Hannibal Sunday school, where his teacher (called Barclay, but actually Richmond) aroused the interest and skepticism of his young pupil by recounting the Genesis story. As Twain remembered it, he asked the teacher if he had ever heard of another woman who "being approached by a serpent, would not excuse herself and break for the nearest timber." Although the question could have been dealt with rather easily by pointing out that the event occurred before God put enmity between women and serpents, the teacher would not answer and instead rebuked Sam for inquiring into such matters. He did, however, tell the boy "the facts of Satan's history," and Sam planned a biography of the devil until Richmond's disapproval cut short the project.[25] It is not likely that the incident happened exactly as Twain recorded it, but it probably is true that the Sunday school planted an early interest in Adam, Eve, and Satan, that trio whose story Twain seemed compelled to tell again and again. The story also brings out a connection between Twain and the pair in Eden; as he once wrote Mrs. Fairbanks, "I *will* be more reverential, if you want me to, though I tell you it don't jibe with my principles. There is a fascination about meddling with forbidden things" (*Mrs. Fairbanks*, 107).

One of the reasons for Twain's extraordinary attraction to Adam was his perception of the similarity of their situations, a similarity which may be observed in *Tom Sawyer*, where Twain, as author, looking back to his youth in Hannibal-St. Petersburg, seems much like an older Adam recalling Eden. Though he expressed the desire to do so, Twain knew he could never go back and be a boy again.

The only way in which Twain could go back to that early Hannibal at all was through writing fiction about it, and this he began to do in *Tom Sawyer* (1876). As he described it in the novel, St. Petersburg was a kind of ideal realm. Everywhere in the picture there is present what Dixon Wecter called "the idealistic haze with which Mark so often invested his Hannibal."[26] Sex and real work are as lacking as in Eden. The boys' misdeeds are not bad, but, as Aunt Polly says, "only mischeevous." If there is any serpent lurking about, it must be either Injun Joe or the threat of death in the cave. Both are successfully overcome.

Twain once wrote of the similarity between himself and Adam disparadised. Jenny Stevens Boardman, the daughter of the old Hannibal jeweler, had reminisced to him about the old days in their town, and to her he replied: "You have spirited me back to a vanished world and the companionship of phantoms ... in thinking of it, dreaming over it, I have seemed like some banished Adam who is revisiting his half-forgotten Paradise and wondering how the arid outside world could ever have seemed green and fair to him."[27] Without mentioning Adam, Twain had written to William Dean Howells in much the same vein, confessing that his friend's *Indian Summer* "makes a body laugh all the time, & cry inside, & feel so old & so forlorn; & gives him gracious glimpses of his lost youth that fill him with a measureless regret, & build up in him a cloudy sense of his having been a prince, once, in some enchanted far-off land, & of being in exile now, & desolate—& lord, no chance to ever get back there again! That is the thing that hurts."[28] Twain was not yet fifty when he penned those lines; fifteen years later he reminisced to the wife of his old friend, Will Bowen: "Those were pleasant days; none since have been so pleasant, none so well worth living over again. ... I should greatly like to re-live my youth, & then get drowned. I should like to call back Will Bowen & John Garth & the others, & live the life, & be as we were, & make holiday until 15, then all drown together."[29]

If Twain had carried out an early scheme for writing Tom Sawyer's life, we might have seen that Tom too found that the early paradise was forever lost. One of his outlines reads: "1, Boyhood & youth; 2 y & early manh; 3 the Battle of Life in many lands; 4 (age 37 to [40?],) return & meet grown babies & toothless old drivelers who were the grandees of his boyhood. The Adored Unknown a [illegible] faded old maid & full of rasping, puritanical vinegar piety."[30] Since Twain abandoned plans for carrying Tom beyond the first of these stages, the book stands in contrast to *Huckleberry Finn*, which takes a much harder look at life, particularly in its middle section, when Huck and Jim are drifting down the river on their raft and running into all sorts of danger from the people they encounter. If Tom was like a young Adam in Paradise, Huck was more like a Daniel in a den of lions.

It was not to Hannibal alone that Twain looked back as at an Eden from which he was forever banished. By 1895 he could view the family's life at the Hartford house in the 1870s and 1880s in the same manner. Livy and the children were abroad and had been for several years when Twain once more visited the house, just as it was beginning to be occupied by the Calvin Day family. Rhapsodically he compared it with the living quarters the family had been occupying abroad: "How ugly, tasteless, repulsive, are all the domestic interiors I have ever seen in Europe compared with the perfect taste of this ground floor, with its delicious dream of harmonious color, and its all-pervading spirit of peace and serenity and deep contentment. ... It is the loveliest home that ever was."

Invoking his familiar image of the dream, he declared to his wife that "it seemed as if I had burst awake out of a hellish dream, and had never been away, and that you would come drifting down out of those dainty upper regions with the little children tagging after you" (*Love Letters*, 312). In spite of his hopes, and Livy's, the family was never to live in the house again and never to know the happiness which had been theirs. In another year his favorite daughter, Susy, would be dead.

In *Tom Sawyer* no specific mention is made of Adam, Eden, or the fall. But in other Twain writings the persons and events of the first chapters of Genesis are prominent indeed; surely no other American author has ever thought and written so much about them. At first Twain's approach was basically humorous. In the 1870s, for instance, he conceived the idea of erecting a monument to Adam in Livy's hometown of Elmira, New York. This was while Darwin was shaking the world with his evolutionary theory, and Twain's argument was that Adam would soon be replaced by the monkey and forgotten.[31] Bankers became interested in the idea for the commercial advantage to Elmira which might be in it, and designs were made for the memorial. Twain drew up a petition to Congress, asking permission for the city to erect a monument "in memory of Adam, the father of mankind" after "6,000 years of unappreciation."[32] The petition urged that Adam's "labors were not in behalf of one locality, but for the extension of humanity at large and the blessings which go therewith" (*Biography*, 1648). Congress, however, never got a chance to take action; for the gentleman to whom the petition was sent refused to present it (*Writings*, XXIV, 236). Twain once tried to make literary capital of the idea by using it as the basis of a story. To be called "The Adam Monument," the tale's chief character was, as Dixon Wecter said, "an elder reincarnation" of that Captain Ned Wakeman whom Twain used under the names of Capt. Hurricane Jones, Ned Blakely, and Capt. Stormfield (*Report from Paradise*, xii).

The Adam monument was mentioned in a speech on Adam delivered on some unknown occasion during the 1880s. Once more Twain lamented Adam's having been neglected and ignored, particularly as a subject for banquet toasts. "Considering what we and the whole world owe him," Twain affirmed, "he ought to be in the list."[33] In the vein of *Innocents Abroad*, Twain claimed Adam as "a relative of mine ... the only solitary celebrity in our family." And then, more in the mood of certain *Pudd'nhead Wilson* maxims, he observed that we owe to Adam the two most precious things we have—life and death.[34] But such serious thought lasted only a moment. Adam was, he went on, "a good citizen; a good husband at a time when he was not married; a good father at a time when he had to guess his way, having never been young himself; and would have been a good son if he had had the chance" (*Speeches*, 96). As for his indiscretion in the Garden of Eden, Twain appeared unmoved by the criticism so often leveled at Adam for yielding to sin. He is, Twain proclaimed, "without a stain upon his name, unless it was a stain to take one apple when most of us would have taken the whole crop" (*Speeches*, 97).

The prevailing mood of these pieces about Adam, then, is light and playful. Mainly the humorous possibilities in Adam had appealed to Twain, and the same can be said for *Extracts from Adam's Diary*. Both Twain and Livy were especially well pleased with the diary. To Fred J. Hall he wrote: "The Diary is a gem, if I *do* say it myself that shouldn't" (*Letters*, II, 581). And to Mrs. Fairbanks he chuckled: "*Livy Clemens* has read the Diary of Adam and *approves* it" (*Mrs. Fairbanks*, 270). The piece first appeared in *The Niagara Book*, prepared as a souvenir for sale at the Buffalo World's Fair of 1893, and then in book form in 1904.[35]

The diary begins at some unspecified time after the creation of woman. It cannot be very long afterwards, for Adam refers to Eve as "the new creature" and at first regards her as one of the animals. The narrative continues through the fall to ten years after the birth of Abel, sometime before his murder by Cain. Twain manages to gloss over the events on which he would focus so sharply in his unpublished writings: God's command, the temptation, the fall itself, the murder of Abel. The name of God does not even occur, nor is there any but the most oblique reference to him. It might seem at first thought impossible to tell such a story without introducing God, but Twain manages it. His reason for so doing must have been to maintain the light tone and avoid adverse criticism for bringing God into so flippant a book.

Placing Eden in the United States and having it include Niagara Falls—an idea not present in Twain's original version—was only the first of Twain's departures from the biblical story. Adam, for instance, complains that he never gets a chance to name anything; the new creature "names everything that comes along before I can get in a protest" (*Writings*, XXIII, 260). In Genesis 2, Adam did all the naming, Eve having not yet been created. As Adam tells it, Eve hankered after the forbidden fruit long before the serpent came along to extoll its virtues. "This morning," he writes, "found the new creature trying to clod apples out of that forbidden tree" (262). Adam reports that animals such as lions and tigers live on grass and flowers and eat no meat at all, for to do so would involve the death of something, and death has not yet come into their world (263–64). The Bible never says that the animals were exempt from death prior to the fall. According to Twain's Adam, every beast began destroying its neighbor at the instant Eve ate the fruit; but the Bible gives no indication that the fall had such a result. Such a notion is found, however, in Milton and earlier in the writings of the church fathers.

Eve eats the fruit partly because of the snake's promise that she will receive "a great and fine and noble education" and partly because of Adam's warning that to eat will bring death into the world. In her twisted reasoning, she believes that death would be a good thing since it would provide proper food for the lions, tigers, and buzzards (265). The reader can make no mistake; the point about God's prohibition which Twain later hammered home incessantly is lacking here: Adam and Eve know what "death" means. They have understood the command given them and have at least some idea of the consequences of disobedience. Adam himself eats the fruit purely because of hunger. It is against his principles, but he observes that "principles have no real force except when one is well fed"(266). This is perhaps the most serious idea the book contains. In the Genesis account, Eve blames the serpent for her wrongdoing, but here she blames Adam, and is successful in convincing him that it is one of his jokes, or chestnuts—the snake has revealed to her that chestnuts are really the forbidden fruit— that is really responsible. Adam does not blame Eve, as he does in Genesis, and the accusations are not made before God. Twain does follow the Bible in having

Adam and Eve recognize their nakedness, but it is Eve who makes clothes for them instead of God.

The remainder of the diary is taken up with the birth of Cain and Abel and the attempts by Adam to discover precisely what they are—whether fish, kangaroo, or bear. All of this is purely humorous, with the exception of the last paragraph, which is similar in tone to parts of *Eve's Diary* and quite unlike anything that Adam had written previously: "After all these years, I see that I was mistaken about Eve in the beginning; it is better to live outside the Garden with her than inside it without her. At first I thought she talked too much; but now I should be sorry to have that voice fall silent and pass out of my life. Blessed be the chestnut that brought us near together and taught me to know the goodness of her heart and the sweetness of her spirit!" (275). If there were some unorthodox opinions expressed in that paragraph, most readers would not be able to find them for the sentiment.

Twain thought about further versions of the diary. On July 30, 1893, only a short time after he had completed the work just considered, he proposed to "tackle Adam once more, and do him in a kind of friendly and respectful way that will commend him to the Sunday schools. I've been thinking out his first life-days to-day and framing his childish and ignorant impressions and opinions for him" (*Letters*, II, 591–92). The implication here is that *Adam's Diary* does not present a character who can be commended to the Sunday schools, but this was surely not because of any disrespect shown the Bible or any criticism made of it. Such things do not appear in *Adam's Diary*.

In 1905, after writing *Eve's Diary*, Twain reread Adam's. It turned his stomach, so he said, because it was not literature. It had been "degraded to an advertisement of the Buffalo Fair." Determined to make something really good out of it, he struck out some 700 words and inserted about 650 words of new material. Now he thought the book "*dam* good—sixty times as good as it ever was before" (*Letters,* II, 775). The 1906 publication of *Adam's Diary* was not, however, this revision but the 1893 text.[36]

Although written more than ten years later, *Eve's Diary* has a close affinity in subject and tone with the diary of Adam. Twain himself hoped the two would appear together to help the reader see the connections between them. As he put it, Eve was using Adam's diary as her unwitting text (*Letters,* II, 775). They first appeared side by side in *The $30,000 Bequest* (1906).

Eve's Diary was written during the summer of 1905, one year after Livy's death, and that fact added somewhat to the sentimental quality of its last pages. Paine called it "that beautiful fancy" and described it as conveying Twain's "love, his worship, and his tenderness for the one he had laid away." Emphasizing the connection between Twain and the first man, Paine went on to say that Twain had "created Adam in his own image; and his rare Eve is no less the companion with whom, half a lifetime before, he had begun the marriage journey" (*Biography,* 1225–26). Something of Twain's tender feeling for the book can be grasped from his instructions that the illustrations—unlike those the same artist had done for *Adam's Diary*—be without humor (Johnson, 85), and by his confiding to Frederick Duneka, "Eve's Diary is Eve's love-story but we will not name it that" (*Letters,* II, 775).

Eve begins her diary on the day after she was created. Like Adam's, it is full of humorous incongruity, as when she remarks in regard to "the rest of the experiment," later to be identified as Adam, that "some instinct tells me that eternal vigilance is the price of supremacy" (*Writings*, XXIV, 288–89). Niagara is no longer specifically mentioned, but Eve does say that she has tried to persuade Adam to stop going over the falls (301).

Numerous embellishments on the biblical account originally found in *Adam's Diary* appear here as well. Tigers live on strawberries, and Eve is capable of sin before the fall. Speaking of the beauty of the moon, she writes that "it would not be safe to trust me with a moon that belonged to another person and that person didn't know I had it. I could give up a moon that I found in the daytime, because I should be afraid some-one was looking" (288–89). It doesn't sound as if an apple could teach her much.

And then there are the amusing correspondences with *Adam's Diary*. Adam had at first regarded Eve as one of the other animals. She classes him as one of the reptiles. The naming of the animals had been a sore spot for Adam; he was chagrined at Eve's taking over the job. But as she tells it, he was glad to have it off his hands and is "evidently very grateful." Besides, Eve adds, "He can't think of a rational name to save him." Eve seems to have a natural gift at animal identifica-tion, for as she said earlier, "I had never seen a tiger before, but I knew them in a minute by the stripes." And as for Eve's trying to clod apples out of the for-bidden tree, she now reveals that she was trying to get them for Adam. She knows that he has warned her she will come to harm, but she does not worry: "so I come to harm pleasing him, why shall I care for that harm?" One notable difference between the two diaries is that while Adam never referred to God, Eve does mention "the Giver of it all" once, and on two oc-casions even uses the name "God."

There is in the midst of *Eve's Diary* a section printed in italics and headed "Extract from Adam's Diary." Apparently Twain wrote this for a revised version of *Adam's Diary* but then changed his mind and decided to retain the text of 1893. Not wanting to lose the new material, he inserted it in *Eve's Diary*. It consists mainly of Adam's description of Eve, with hints of his growing attraction to her, and tells his story of her affection for the brontosaurus.

As in *Adam's Diary*, the actual scene of the temptation and fall is not described. Adam mentioned Eve's taking up with a snake (never identified as Satan), but we get nothing of this in her diary. We do get an insight into her boundless curiosity and love of experimentation, however, and one might easily infer that the fall came about as a direct result. The serpent, if he did put in an appearance, was really superfluous. Twain gets over the fall simply by having the diary stop before it occurs and then take up sometime thereafter.

In some respects it is a changed Eve that figures in the sections headed "After the Fall" and "Forty Years Later." Like Adam, she finds that having a mate is better than being in the garden without one: "The Garden is lost, but I have found *him*, and am content." She prays that they may die together, and if that cannot be, that she will be the first to go. Her second wish is granted and the last line is spoken by Adam standing at her grave, as Twain had stood at Livy's: "Wheresoever she was, *there* was Eden."[37] Never again would Twain be able with such feeling and without bitterness to write of the first couple the world had ever known.

The slight touches of heresy tinging these documents are almost lost in the wealth of humor and senti-

ment which Twain put into them. Writing for a public whose orthodoxy he overestimated, he apparently
felt it necessary to suppress the angry charges which
he hurled in his unpublished writings. In only two
published works do we find a hint of Twain's less respectable, less orthodox ideas about what took place in
the Garden of Eden, and in both cases these are well
disguised with humor.

One of the most popular features of the novel
Pudd'nhead Wilson (1894) was the epigram at the
opening of each chapter, ostensibly taken from a cal-
endar prepared by the title character. Several concerned Adam and Eve, among them this one: "Adam
was but human—this explains it all. He did not want
the apple for the apple's sake, he wanted it only because it was forbidden. The mistake was in not forbid-
ding the serpent; then he would have eaten the serpent" (*Writings,* XIV, 19). Readers may well have
laughed and gone on, perhaps saying to themselves,
"That's a pretty good one." And too, this was supposed to be Pudd'nhead's saying, not Twain's. But beneath the humor lies first the suggestion that Adam
could not have chosen abstinence because of his God-
given nature and second a hint that God was rather
foolish to expect the outcome to be otherwise. These
rebellious notions were given more prominence in
"The Turning-Point of My Life." Here Twain with
his deterministic reasoning pointed out another cause
of his interest in Eden and the fall. It was there, he
wrote, "that the first link was forged of the chain that
was ultimately to lead to the emptying of me into the
literary guild." Adam's temperament, he went on, was
God's first command and the only one Adam could
not disobey. The contradictory command to let the
fruit alone was certain to be disobeyed, for no one

may go against his nature, no matter how much he is ordered to do so: "The law of the tiger's temperament is, Thou shalt kill; the law of the sheep's temperament is, Thou shalt not kill. To issue later commands requiring the tiger to let the fat stranger alone, and requiring the sheep to imbue its hands in the blood of the lion is not worth while, for those commands *can't* be obeyed. They would invite to violations of the law of *temperament*, which is supreme, and takes precedence of all other authorities" (*Complete Essays,* 484–85). This was going pretty far toward challenging the customary assumption that Adam and Eve had complete freedom to choose right or wrong, but Twain smoothed it over with a burst of fantasy and humor: "What I cannot help wishing is, that Adam and Eve had been postponed, and Martin Luther and Joan of Arc put in their place. ... By neither sugary persuasions nor by hell fire could Satan have beguiled *them* to eat the apple. There would have been results! Indeed, yes. The apple would be intact to-day; there would be no human race; there would be no *you;* there would be no *me.* And the old, old creation-dawn scheme of ultimately launching me into the literary guild would have been defeated" (485). Naturally some readers would object to the mild contradictions of the Bible found in *Adam's Diary, Eve's Diary,* and "The Turning-Point of My Life." To most they must have seemed rather innocent toying with biblical themes. And they were— in spite of a few suggestions of the more serious criticism which Twain had thought out but had not decided to make public. Much more specific challenges to biblical facts and doctrines came in the writings which have appeared since his death.

The first group of these writings was published by Paine in *Europe and Elsewhere* (1923). Here the biblical fantasies were more pointed, but they appeared sufficiently mild to Paine, often a bit squeamish about Twain's indiscretions, that he could bring himself to publish them. One such sketch is called "Adam's Soliloquy," though the subject comes nearer being the flood than the fall. The setting is not Eden but New York City, and the time is the present. It has been 300,000 years since Adam's first child was born and 30,000 years since the flood.[38] The soliloquy is in two sections, the first taking place at the American Museum of Natural History and the second in Central Park. The first shows Twain using the flood story as a vehicle to discredit the Bible and so will not be dealt with at present. The second section, more concerned with the story itself and less with the presentation of Twain's beliefs, demonstrates that there are light passages in the works not published until after 1910. Its humor is akin to that of the Adam passage in *Innocents Abroad:* both use the idea that Adam, as the first man, is related to everyone living upon the earth. Sitting leisurely on a park bench, Adam looks about him, reflecting that all who are passing are "blood kin," and when a lady declares that she would be thrown into fits by seeing the original Adam, he reminds her that she should not be alarmed at meeting a distant relative. To Adam's delight, she thinks the remark "prodigiously funny."

In a more serious vein are the retellings of the fall, "That Day in Eden" and "Eve Speaks." The former introduced a new viewpoint: Satan was allowed to give his side, and the piece was subtitled "Passage from Satan's Diary."[39] Although Twain had managed to keep Satan out of the diaries of Adam and Eve, he had long been fascinated by him. In an autobiographical entry of 1897–1898, he wrote: "And I have always felt friendly toward Satan. Of course that is ancestral; it must be in the blood, for I could not have originated it."[40] In his essay "Concerning the Jews," published in *Harper's Magazine* for September 1899, Twain had again spoken highly of the Prince of Darkness: "We may not pay him reverence, for that would be indiscreet, but we can at least respect his talents. A person who has for untold centuries maintained the imposing position of spiritual head of four-fifths of the human race, and political head of the whole of it, must be granted the possession of executive abilities of the loftiest order. ... I would rather see him and shake him by the tail than any other member of the European Concert."[41] Prior to his writing "That Day in Eden," Twain had done several pieces in which Satan figured prominently. Among these were the 1897 "Letters to Satan," subtitled "Swiss Glimpses," supposed to be a report by Twain to Satan regarding the former's travels (*Europe*, 211–20); the 1904 "Sold to Satan," in which he plays Faust, having determined to sell his soul (*Europe*, 326–38); and "A Humane Word from Satan," ostensibly a letter from Satan to *Harper's Weekly*, in which it appeared April 8, 1905.[42]

Twain had shown an interest in Satan's relatives too. In 1898 he recorded in his notebook an idea for a story about "Little Satan, Jr." who went to school at Hannibal (*Notebook*, 369). Further developed, the idea became one of the versions of "The Mysterious Stranger." In the published, or "Eseldorf" version, however, it is not Satan's son but his nephew whom we meet. He bears the name Satan but in a remarkable Twain embellishment on the Bible makes it clear he is not the one who sinned: "It was only he that I was named for who ate of the fruit of the tree and then beguiled the man and the woman with it." (*Complete*

Short Stories, 606). There is nothing in Genesis or elsewhere in Twain which mentions such an act.

"That Day in Eden (Passage from Satan's Diary)," relates how Adam and Eve came to eat the apple and thus to bring the moral sense and death into the world. What Twain had kept dark in the diaries of Adam and Eve he now brought into the spotlight, and this time his purpose was not comedy but a serious attack on either God or the Bible, or both. Two verses from the Bible are central to the piece and to much of Twain's subsequent treatment of the fall: "And the Lord God commanded the man, saying, Of every tree of the garden thou mayest freely eat: But of the tree of the knowledge of good and evil, thou shalt not eat of it: for in the day that thou eatest thereof thou shalt surely die" (Genesis 2:16–17). The whole point of "That Day in Eden" is that God was stupid to utter such a command, for it was totally incomprehensible to Adam, and to Eve when he told her of it.[43] Since it had no meaning for the pair, one could not reasonably expect that it would be obeyed. Further inferences, though not spelled out, are apparent: to punish the disobedience of Adam and Eve was unfair and unjust, and the greatest injustice of all was to punish mankind in general for that one uncomprehending act on that one day near the beginning of time. If the reader should protest that the story of Adam and Eve was not literally true, Twain could simply transfer the stupidity from God to the Bible. If God did not give the absurd command quoted, then it was absurd of the Bible to say that he did. Either way Twain was saying something that would have been startling and disturbing to the Christians of his day if it had been available to them.

"That Day in Eden" is supposed to have been written by Satan on the day of the fall. The opening part of the narration depicts the innocence of Adam and Eve in their original state and their bewilderment over the strange words in the prohibition which God had given them. Most of the diary passage consists of a dialogue between Satan and Eve, as the former tries to explain the words God had used. He finds the effort totally futile, for as he says, "Things which are outside of our orbit—our own particular world—things which by our constitution and equipment we are unable to see, or feel, or otherwise experience—*cannot be made comprehensible to us in words*" (*Europe*, 341). Satan, though he modestly refrains from saying so, is wiser than God. A second major Twain idea is introduced in Satan's criticism of the moral sense. Twain had frequently heard preachers praise the wonderful gift of the moral sense, but he had Satan tell Eve that it is "a degradation, a disaster. Without it one cannot do wrong; with it, one can. Therefore it has but one office, only one—to teach how to do wrong ... wrong cannot exist until the Moral Sense brings it into being" (344). Twain would keep hammering this point home for the remainder of his life.[44]

The fall occurs when Satan tells Eve that she can have the moral sense by eating the fruit of the tree. She eats and is at once aware of her degradation and loss of modesty. In another Twain improvement of Genesis, she becomes an old woman, with gray hair and wrinkles. Adam "loyally and bravely" eats the apple too and they go their way.

The action of "Eve Speaks" follows closely upon that of "That Day in Eden" and develops the same themes.[45] The time is three months after the expulsion from Eden. Eve begins with the insistence that she and Adam had done no harm and should not have been punished: "We could not know it was wrong to disobey the command, for the words were strange to us and we did not understand them." Picking up a point not made in Satan's version of the story, Twain had her go on to argue: "We did not know right from wrong—how should we know? We could not, without the Moral Sense; it was not possible. If we had been given the Moral Sense first—ah, that would have been fairer, that would have been kinder; then we should be to blame if we disobeyed" (*Europe*, 347). And Twain proceeds, using Eve as his mouthpiece for a denunciation of the moral sense.

But then Twain gives us something new—the moment at which Eve first senses the meaning of that "death" of which God had spoken in his command. Abel[46] has been murdered by Cain, but Adam and Eve at first only suppose him to be asleep. Gradually realization comes, and Eve's final words are: "Oh, is it that long sleep—is it death? And will he wake no more?" (*Europe*, 350). Twain leaves the reader to make the inference that had Eve known at the beginning what "death" meant, she would never have eaten the fruit of the forbidden tree. It is Satan who has the last word, in a paragraph headed "From Satan's Diary." Death has entered the world, he writes. The product of the moral sense is complete. And then in the mood of Pudd'nhead Wilson's maxim that Adam's most beneficent deed was to bring death into the world he concludes: "The Family think ill of death— they will change their minds" (350). Obviously the tone and thought here are a world away from the simple humor of *Adam's Diary*, and Twain was to become still more serious in the biblical fantasies which did not find publication until *Letters from the Earth* (1962).

Three Biblical Images

"Eve's Autobiography" (c. 1905–1906) has within it humorous elements as well as serious, partaking of the characteristics of both *Eve's Diary* and "Eve Speaks." A comparatively long work—Bernard DeVoto omitted some 4,100 words of it when he edited it for *Letters from the Earth*[47]—it is supposed to have been written by Eve sometime after the year 900 A.C. (after the creation), as the flood draws nearer. (By this time, Twain was dating the flood as 920 A.C.) In her autobiography, Eve, like Twain, looks back at her idyllic life before the fall. As a matter of fact, the fall is never described in the manuscript; after having written nine thousand words, Twain still had not gotten Eve out of Eden, and at that point he abandoned the project.

The autobiography is most like the diaries of Adam and Eve in its humorous accounts of the couple's attempt to understand their surroundings. Their scientific interest is prominent; their conclusions sometimes correct and sometimes quite humorously wrong. Incongruous names are introduced: there is a lion called William McKinley and two of the sisters of Cain and Abel are named Gladys and Edwina. As in the diaries, William McKinley and his fellows content themselves with cabbages, while Bengal tigers are reportedly fond of strawberries and onions.[48] There is a prehistoric beast too. In *Eve's Diary* it had been a brontosaurus; here it is a pterodactyl, called Terry for short. Once again the birth of children presents a puzzle. As in *Adam's Diary*, numerous theories are formulated and discarded as Adam tries to determine "what kind of bird or reptile or quadruped it was." But, whereas in the diaries there were no births until after Adam and Eve left the garden, here they have nine children before the fall takes place.

The serious part of "Eve's Autobiography" is a presentation of the same point emphasized in "That Day in Eden" and "Eve Speaks," that God's command was incomprehensible. Eve recalls how Adam confessed to her that he had no idea as to the meaning of "good," "evil," and "death." Twain does not dwell on the point, though, and the whole autobiography is much more like the diaries than like the narratives which first appeared in *Europe and Elsewhere*.

In "Letters from the Earth" (the first section of the book now bearing that title) written about 1909, Satan is banished from heaven and visits the earth to "see how the Human-Race experiment was coming along." To his friends the angels Michael and Gabriel, Satan writes a series of letters—thus the title—describing the foolishness and pettiness of man and discussing in considerable detail the book man values most, the Bible. Here there was humor, but not humor for its own sake; Twain was bringing his biggest guns to bear on the Bible and the Christian religion.

As Satan narrates the story of the fall, he makes the point heard time and again, that God was insane to expect Adam and Eve to obey a command they could not understand: "inasmuch as they had never seen a sample of death they could not possibly know what he meant" (*LE*, 16). The serpent enters the picture, walking upright, a detail Twain had missed before, presumably based on the fact that God's curse upon him would have no meaning if he had always crawled on the ground. Incidentally, Satan, writing the letter, makes no mention of his own involvement in this episode. Following Genesis, he does not connect the serpent and Satan.

Adam and Eve eat the fruit, and Twain gets off a few more blasts at the moral sense. This time the main knowledge they get from eating it is "the art and mystery of sexual intercourse." That this runs directly contrary to most of his previous pictures of life in Eden disturbs Twain not a whit. He goes right along, even improving Genesis a little by having Adam and Eve engaged in sex at the moment God comes walking in the Garden. The blame for the fall is clearly fixed on God himself: "the only person responsible for the couple's offense escaped; and not only escaped but became the executioner of the innocent" (*LE,* 17, 19). This was plain language indeed, making explicit what had only been implicit in Twain's previous tellings of the story.

After reporting the birth of Cain and Abel and later the union between the sons of God and the daughters of men, who are described as "those hot young blossoms," Twain (or Satan) goes on to tell of God's decision to destroy mankind, "the only really enlightened and superior idea his Bible has credited him with." Noah and his family, however, were to be saved, providing a third major image—Noah and the coming doom.

In one of his letters to the *Alta California,* sent from Smyrna in 1867, Mark Twain pondered the various theories explaining the presence of three veins of oyster shells on a hill 500 feet above the sea and then put forth a biblical one of his own: "It is just possible that this hill is Mount Ararat, and that Noah's Ark rested here, and he ate oysters and threw the shells overboard. But that will not do, either. There are the three layers again and the solid earth between—and, besides, there were only eight in Noah's family, and they could not have eaten all these oysters in the two or three months they staid on top of that mountain. The beasts —however, it is simply absurd to suppose he didn't know any more than to feed the beasts on oyster suppers. He couldn't afford it, anyhow. He had been out eleven months, and they must have been on short rations for some time."[49] Soon afterwards he visited the traditional site of the tomb of "the honored old navigator" and informed his readers, "Noah's memorable voyage will always possess a living interest for me, henceforward."[50] Though Twain was partly joking, his statement turned out to be true. His interest in Noah was to manifest itself in numerous published and unpublished sketches for the rest of his life. The implication that Noah had not been of interest previously, however, was false. We have already noted his attraction to a phrase from the story, "the fountains of the great deep were broken up,"[51] and during his tour of the Sandwich Islands a visit to the top of Haleakala volcano brought the story to his mind and caused him to imagine a scene not depicted in Genesis: "Standing on that peak, with all the world shut out by that vast plain of clouds, a feeling of loneliness comes over a man which suggests to his mind the last man at the flood, perched high upon the last rock, with nothing visible on any side but a mournful waste of waters, and the ark departing dimly through the distant mists and leaving him to storm and night and solitude and death!"[52] In addition to these briefer references to the flood story, Twain was in the summer of 1866 contemplating a longer sketch on the subject; en route from Honolulu to San Francisco he jotted down an idea in his notebook: "Conversation between the carpenters of Noah's Ark, laughing at him for an old visionary" (*Notebook*, 26). It is hard to tell from that brief note whether Twain's concept of the unheeded prophet of doom was humorous or serious. He never wrote a sketch in precisely that form, and it was several years before he did anything extensive concerning Noah, though he from time to time used comparisons with the flood story, as when he asked Mrs. Fairbanks —referring to the end of the *Quaker City* excursion— "Why grieve that the ark hath rested upon Ararat & the animals departed two by two to be seen no more of Noah & his sons?" (*Mrs. Fairbanks*, 7).

The first biblical fantasy involving Noah which is of any length is one which appeared in Twain's Buffalo *Express* with the signature "Hy Slocum." Although some of the Twain attributions in Henry Duskis's collection of Buffalo *Express* material[53] appear doubtful, here several factors point to Twain's authorship: the previous use he had made of the subject matter; the treatment given the subject, quite similar to that in some of the *Quaker City* letters; and the fact that he was planning a book on the subject.

In this sketch Noah is pictured landing at Ararat surrounded by "a swarm of vociferous hack drivers and hotel runners." No explanation is offered as to how they survived the flood. Noah speaks in a blend of biblical language and contemporary usage: "I am a man of grace, but if any among ye remaineth two minutes, him will I chastise! *You hear me!*" They say to themselves, "Verily, the old man is a knocker! Let us depart! Golah!" (*Forgotten Writings*, 138). Nothing could be more like the style of such Twain pieces as the story of the seven sleepers, which appeared first in an *Alta* letter and was then revised for *Innocents Abroad*. A pun on Ham's name, such as Twain once used in a Lick House banquet menu,[54] appears: Noah's chagrin at failing to kick a "yaller dog" is aggravated by Ham's smile, which "never was cured ... until, in the process of mummification, they converted him into a sugar cured Ham" (*Forgotten Writings*, 139). As in Twain's story of Joseph for the *Alta California*, there are references to other parts of the Bible. The yaller dog is termed "an Ishmaelite among dogs," and the author reports that when tin cans are tied to his tail he "flees from the wrath to come."[55]

That Twain wrote the fantasy appears the more probable because he was at work on a Noah book during this period, the one he had been contemplating since he left Hawaii. On January 22, 1870, two months after the piece just described appeared in the *Express*, Twain wrote his publisher: "I mean to take plenty of time & pains with the Noah's Ark book— maybe it will be several years before it is *all* written— but it will be a perfect lightning-striker when it *is* done."[56] Elisha Bliss, however, never got the chance to publish the new book. Like so many other Twain projects, it was never completed. In 1909 he began it again, "for recreation," he said, and without "any intention of carrying it to a finish—or even to the end of the first chapter, in fact."[57]

Paine says that Twain's idea was "to detail the cruise of the Ark in diaries kept by various members of it— Shem, Ham, and the others."[58] This was the first of the several occasions on which Twain employed the notion of a journal kept by a biblical character. Paine quotes some excerpts from what was perhaps intended to be only a part of a larger work and identifies these as "Shem's Diary," written in Buffalo in 1870, the year of Twain's marriage. It is harmless fun, with such bits as Shem's dislike of Methuselah for still calling him "Shemmy," just as he had when he was "a child of sixty."[59] The idea that all things were then as they are now was, however, one which Twain came to use with increasing seriousness in his later biblical pieces.

If this mild sketch was supposed to be Twain's "perfect lightning-striker," it did not come off. It might well be, of course, that he had second thoughts about the nature of the proposed book. This was, after all, less than a month before his marriage, when he was supposed to be reforming. One cannot be sure what he meant by the term "lightning-striker," but an obvious inference is that he was out to shake up the biblical literalists. Despite Twain's claim in a *Quaker City* letter that his reverence for the scriptures was "pretty firmly grounded" (*Traveling*, 166), it appears that his irreverence was much more firmly established.

The one extensive treatment of Noah which Twain published during his lifetime was a section titled "Noah's Ark" in "About All Kinds of Ships."[60] Consisting of a conversation between Noah and a ship inspector, its main point was that Noah would not be permitted to sail under present-day regulations. He had no rudder, anchor, or life preservers, his crew was too small, and so on. The answers which Noah gives to the inspector's questions contain many facts and phrases from the biblical account. For instance, Noah states the passengers' ages as from 100 to 600, which is precisely in line with the Genesis chronology, according to which Shem was 100 and Noah 600 at the time of the flood. (One might, of course, suppose from Genesis that Ham and Japheth were younger than 100, but their ages are not specified.) Twain gives some nonbiblical statistics too, as when he has Noah state that the total number of animals on board will be 98,000. And here Twain has a chance to get in some subtle hints as to the absurdity of the ark story, for the inspector remarks that such a menagerie would require at least 1,200 keepers (*Writings*, XXI, 470). Another absurdity appears when Noah answers that water will be obtained from the outside by lowering buckets. The inspector points out that this could not be done because the salt oceans would have mixed with the fresh water to such an extent that all water would be too salty to drink.[61]

Twain's objections to the story also appeared in "Adam's Soliloquy," not published until 1923 (*Europe*, 377–86). Adam, inspecting the Museum of Natural History's dinosaur model, remarks that Noah was unaware that such a creature existed, for it was "not named in his cargo list."[62] Twain believed that if the Bible were truly an accurate record it would have somewhere mentioned the existence of a race of animals no longer to be found upon the earth.

Adam proceeds to recount a conversation with Noah about his eventful voyage, a conversation which, by the way, must have taken place in heaven, since Adam died before the flood and even before Noah was born. According to Noah, it was his "boys" that were partly responsible for what went wrong. In general they did their work well, but they put on board the ark a multitude of useless animals such as flies, mosquitoes, and snakes, at the same time neglecting to collect specimens of many more valuable creatures. Noah further recalled that they lost a good many animals who could not drink the salty water they had as a result of the salt oceans mixing with the fresh water, a point Twain also made in the sketch previously discussed (*Europe*, 379). But all the locusts, grasshoppers, weevils, rats, and cholera germs survived without difficulty. Twain's argument is approximately this: if the Bible is literally true, then something like what Noah related had to happen. Certainly the locusts and grasshoppers were saved. God could have destroyed these harmful creatures, but he did not. He must either be stupid or malevolent—or else the Bible is wrong. Its readers could see this if they would examine it honestly and without preconceived notions. And if it is wrong, of course, it cannot be divinely inspired but must be the product of fallible men, lacking any authority beyond what reason can grant it.

Letters from the Earth offers two views of the flood. One of these, that in the title section, picks up and carries further what Twain had been saying since his "About All Kinds of Ships" article. The ark lacked a rudder, sails, compass, pumps, chart, lead-lines, anchors, and cargo room. Once again the point about the unavailability of fresh water is raised (*LE*, 22). Twain revised statistics upward. Where he had previously fixed the number of animals aboard the ark at 98,000, he now made it 146,000 kinds of birds, beasts, and fresh-water creatures, plus over two million species of insects (23). Later Twain states that Noah took 68 billion flies and forty tons of filth to support them (25). Certain additions to the biblical report are worked in, such as the story of many great animals coming to the ark yet being left behind and that of Noah's having to turn back in order to pick up a fly (24, 25). A similar point was made in "Adam's Soliloquy." With sarcasm and bitterness of a kind not present in his previous biblical fantasies, Twain portrays a scene not described in the Bible, the lamentations of "the multitude of weeping fathers and mothers and frightened little children who were clinging to the wave-washed rocks in the pouring rain and lifting imploring prayers to an All-Just and All-Forgiving and All-Pitying Being who had never answered a prayer since those crags were builded, grain by grain out of the sands, and would still not have answered one when the ages should have crumbled them to sand again."[63]

Twain's attack on the Bible, apparent throughout his accounts of the fall and the flood, becomes so prominent at this point in "Letters from the Earth" that it is only from time to time that the reader hears how Noah's voyage is going. In the ninth of the eleven letters the ark finally lands on Ararat, and Noah becomes drunk from the wine of the vineyard he planted. "The promise was bad," Twain has Satan remark.

In the second view of Noah found in *Letters from the Earth,* particularly in "Papers of the Adam Family," there comes to the fore his role as the prophet of a terrible destruction about to overtake a corrupt civilization. Something of this can be seen in the comparatively early "Methuselah's Diary," supposed to have been written in 747 A.C. As Twain imagines it, the life of that time is remarkably similar to that in nineteenth-century America. The same device had been used in the Buffalo *Express* sketch, but without realizing the effects achieved here. Methuselah tells of tourists who carve their names and addresses on ruins; of plays being performed, including one on "the Driving Forth from Eden"; of ladies with wigs and lap dogs; of missionaries eaten by cannibals; of a baseball game, complete with such expressions as "Three-Base Hit" and "Caught out on a Foul"; of a museum which displays (instead of the True Cross) the True and Original Flaming Sword used in the expulsion from Eden. Twain even planned to have Methuselah set up a republican form of government (as the Connecticut Yankee later intended) and to detail its history, working in numerous elements from contemporary American history whenever there was a good chance for satire. DeVoto tells us that Twain intended to describe such events as the growing up of a bureaucracy, a women's rights crusade, the corruption of the judiciary, and the triumph of the demagogues (*LE*, 68). By introducing such elements into the world of 747 A.C., Twain may seem chiefly to have been striving for the humor of incongruity. But there is always the more serious underlying thought that people do not change very much after all; history repeats itself. Later Twain was to elaborate this as the "law of periodical repetition." Although the corruption of Methuselah's civilization is not dwelt upon, we are reminded that it is a doomed one when Methuselah refers to "that silly deluge whereof overpious fools with ill digestion do prate and prophesy from time to time."[64]

"Methuselah's Diary" was to a considerable extent a humorous work, but when he came to write the later pieces in "Papers of the Adam Family" Twain was in a more serious mood. In a series of passages and extracts he describes the state of the world in 920 A.C. Once again he imagined that civilization had reached a high peak at that time. It had gone through the industrial revolution and now all sorts of inventions had been perfected—ships, the railroad, electricity. Again there are suggestions of the Connecticut Yankee's creation of a modern world in ancient Britain. The similarities between 920 A.C. and the twentieth century are explained through the "law of periodical repetition," which the Mad Philosopher formulates as "Everything which has happened once must happen again and again and again."

This law gave Twain the excuse to introduce into the life of 920 all sorts of correspondences with his own time, including such specifics as the invasion of the Philippines and Theodore Roosevelt's Executive

Order No. 78, relating to soldier pensions (*LE*, 107). Even Mary Baker Eddy's *Science and Health* turns up, identified as "the forgotten book ... with us once more, revised, corrected, and its orgies of style and construction tamed by an educated disciple" (101). Twain risked breaking the mood of the work by such a shot at a current enemy, but he could not resist it. The law of periodical repetition may also explain what is otherwise a startling biblical anachronism. In what is supposed to be a suppressed book of c. 920 this passage occurs: "The sleeping republic awoke at last, but too late. It drove the money-changers from the temple, and put the government into clean hands—but all to no purpose."[65]

The note of doom in this passage sounds louder still in others. In spite of its technological competence, the civilization of 920 is sick and dying. The Mad Philosopher, whom Twain uses for a mouthpiece, analyzes it to Eve,[66] who is now called "the Most Illustrious, Most Powerful, Most Gracious, Most Reverend, her Grandeur, the Acting Head of the Human Race": "It is a civilization which has destroyed the simplicity and repose of life; replaced its contentment, its poetry, its soft romance-dreams and visions with the money-fever, sordid ideals, vulgar ambitions, and the sleep which does not refresh; it has invented a thousand useless luxuries, and turned them into necessities; it has created a thousand vicious appetites and satisfies none of them; it has dethroned God and set up a shekel in His place. ... Your civilization has brought the flood. Noah has said it, and he is preparing (*LE*, 98). There is probably no better statement of Twain's judgment on his own time. Both civilizations—Eve's and his own—were doomed, he thought: hers by the flood[67] and his by some still unknown catastrophe, which the law of periodical repetition would shortly bring to pass.

What began as playful treatment of well-known stories from the Bible went on to become serious statement of Twain's beliefs, with the biblical material serving primarily as a convenient vehicle for conveying the point to the reader. A precise demarcation line between comic and serious biblical fantasies cannot really be drawn. Obviously some, like *Adam's Diary* and *Eve's Diary*, are essentially comic and contain little Twain philosophy or criticism of the Bible. Others, such as "That Day in Eden" and "Eve Speaks," are almost pure seriousness and are primarily criticisms of the biblical stories on which they are based as well as of those who go on believing these stories and teaching them to others. As in so many other writings, Twain was trying to show what could be found in the Bible if readers would only cast aside their pretenses about its being a sacred and inspired book and see what was really there.

Generally speaking, it was about 1893 that more serious elements of criticism began to appear in Twain's biblical fantasies—"Methuselah's Diary" is an exception —and about 1905 or 1906 that humor began to disappear.[68] Correlations between Twain's life and his writings are tenuous, but it can be pointed out that in 1894 the typesetter into which Twain had poured so much money finally failed and he went into bankruptcy. In 1896 came the unexpected death of the oldest daughter Susy, and in 1904 Livy died after twenty-two months of illness.

A further generalization may be ventured: the biblical fantasies Twain published are the most humorous and the least serious. Some of his most serious writing appeared in the posthumous *Europe and Elsewhere.* The selections in *Letters from the Earth* tend to be mixtures of light and serious, and some could have been published immediately after writing except for their fragmentary nature. In the Adam family papers it is society rather than the Bible that is damned, though of course in "Letters from the Earth" itself the Bible is attacked with a vehemence not found elsewhere except in the 1906 autobiographical dictations. That Twain wrote, yet failed to publish, these attacks on the Bible indicates once again his simultaneous desire to criticize and to be approved. Certain of his criticisms of the Bible did appear in print in Twain's lifetime, but these were offset by humor or presented without the emphasis of "Letters from the Earth" or "Eve Speaks."

4.

The Attack On The Bible

THE BIBLE, Mark Twain wrote in the year before his
death, "is full of interest. It has noble poetry in it; and
some clever fables; and some blood-drenched history;
and some good morals; and a wealth of obscenity; and
upwards of a thousand lies" (*LE*, 14). In this one
statement as perhaps nowhere else Twain expressed his
final attitude toward the Bible. It never failed to arouse
his interest and in some respects his admiration, but for
him its bad points so heavily outweighed the good that
he came to rage against it with increasing fervor as he
neared the close of his life.

On the positive side, Twain seems to have admired
what he once called "the quaint, old-fashioned sound
and structure of our King James's translation of the
Scriptures" (*Writings*, VII, 132), even though some
aspects of it became objects of his satire. That the Bible had much real influence upon his own style seems
rather doubtful,[1] but he did appreciate its simplicity
and directness. Once when criticizing long prayers he
asked: "How would it do to be less diffuse? ... How
would it answer to adopt the simplicity and the brev-
ity and the comprehensiveness of the Lord's Prayer as

a model?"[2] *The American Claimant* has an appendix which makes the same point. Headed "Weather for Use in This Book Selected from the Best Authorities," it reprints several flowery, elaborate passages climaxed by "It rained forty days and forty nights.—*Genesis*" (*Writings*, XXI, 231). We know that Twain liked certain biblical passages, some for their beauty ("the shadow of a great rock in a weary land")[3] and others for their moral import. Chief among the latter was the golden rule, which Twain hailed as "Exhibit A in the Church's assets."[4] Twain apparently found praiseworthy such passages as Matthew 25, whose story of the Last Judgment he seems to parallel in Simon Wheeler's dream of heaven.[5] But it is very seldom that Twain is recorded as having made such a remark as one attributed to him by William C. S. Pellowe, who recounted how Twain was visited in London by a British friend. Seeing an open Bible in the room, the friend asked Twain if he were studying it. Replied Twain: "That's a good book ... about the most interesting Book I ever read. ... It beats any novel or history or work of science that I ever tackled. It is full of good stories and philosophy. It suggests lots of ideas, and there's news in it."[6] Never would Twain have spoken of the Bible as did his friend and pastor Joseph Twichell: "if you were to cause the ministry of the Bible that is now going on to cease, a shadow would fall upon the world. To-day it is helping many and many a poor stricken soul to live and not die, to trust and not sink. ... It is helping many a boy away from home to be true to his conscience and his mother. It is pleading with many a youth standing where two ways meet not to yield to the bribes of sin. It is brightening many a hard and toilsome lot. It is cheering many a sick-chamber, and smoothing many a dying pillow. It would desolate ten thousands of hearts to take it away; and remove a mighty safeguard from ten thousands more."[7] One could almost believe this a Twain parody of the respectable, pious, sentimental views of the dominant culture.

In 1887 Twain complained to Howells about people who pretend that they still hold at fifty the same beliefs about the Bible they had as younger people and even as children: "I wonder how they can lie so. It comes of practice, no doubt. They would not say that of Dickens's or Scott's books. *Nothing* remains the same ... it has always *shrunk*. ... Shrunk how? Why, to its correct dimensions; the *house* hasn't altered: this is the first time it has been in focus."[8] Judging by what he says in *Innocents Abroad* of his disillusionment with the Holy Land, Twain too had the experience of finding that the Bible had shrunk. But it is difficult to discover a time when Twain possessed a real awe and admiration for the Bible, when he thought it truly large. If he ever had such feelings they must have departed with early childhood, for his adult life, and even early years, were to a high degree informed by skepticism.

In 1906 Twain was working steadily on his autobiography, dictating portions nearly every day. For five days in June, while in Dublin, New Hampshire, he dictated chapters pertaining to the Bible and the Christian religion which he thought so scandalous they could not see print for at least a century. To Howells he wrote: "To-morrow I mean to dictate a chapter which will get my heirs & assigns burnt alive if they venture to print it this side of 2006 A.D.—which I judge they won't. There'll be lots of such chapters if I live 3 or 4 years longer. The edition of A.D. 2006 will make a stir when it comes out. I shall be hovering around taking notice, along with other dead pals. You

are invited."[9] The promised stir, needless to say, did not materialize when the dictations were printed in 1963.[10]

In the dictation Twain stressed the difference between the Bible God and the real God, describing the former as vindictive, unjust, ungenerous, pitiless, vengeful, cruel, and a punisher of the innocent. This he had done before; but now he confessed that "the Real God, the genuine God" is not much more appealing. Not interested in the human race, he is neither just, kind, nor merciful. He answers no prayers. Yet it cannot be said that he is really indifferent to man, as had been suggested in "If I Could Be There." It is he who established the exact and inflexible law which governs the world and according to which all creatures must suffer pain and misery. Thus he alone, by Twain's reasoning, is responsible for the evils that beset mankind.[11]

The parts of the five dictations most calculated to shock the readers of 2006, or 2406, were a special stress on the cruelty of the Bible God and a forthright denial of the virgin birth. With fervor Twain painted a God "charged and overcharged with evil impulses far beyond the human limit" and "a personage whom no one, perhaps, would desire to associate with now that Nero and Caligula are dead." A few sentences later he was announcing that Nero was "an angel of light and leading" alongside the Bible God ("Reflections," 332). After criticizing the lack of originality in the doctrine of the virgin birth, Twain went on to suggest it was nothing but a story invented by Mary to conceal from Joseph her indiscretions. To top it all off, he declared that "you couldn't purify a tomcat by the Immaculate Conception process" (335–38).

A final statement on the Bible and its God came in

"Letters from the Earth." It too was written with the intention that it be suppressed for a long time. To a friend Twain wrote: "This book will never be published—in fact it couldn't be, because it would be felony to soil the mails with it, for it has much Holy Scripture in it of the kind that ... can't properly be read aloud, except from the pulpit and in family worship" (*Letters*, II, 834). What he probably had in mind were the various references to sexual intercourse and bodily processes of elimination. The spirit which prompted him to write *1601* was at work here too; he seems to have enjoyed writing something shocking, being at the same time secure in the knowledge that it would not be published.

Though much of "Letters from the Earth" became a retelling of the first few chapters of Genesis, Twain also paid his respects to the New Testament, disputing the common notion that Jesus appears "sweet, gentle, merciful, forgiving" in it. Above all, he could not forgive Christ for having invented hell (*LE*, 45).

Twain never sympathized with those persons who believe that a little Scripture is like seasoning, that it needs to be sprinkled around here and there in conversation in order to improve its flavor. Such persons are inclined to feel that they are just a little better for having quoted Scripture and that everyone else should recognize their superior standing. The reverse of the situation is that gullible people believe that a man who can quote Scripture must be a good man and therefore his acts need not be examined with a critical eye.

In the world with which Twain most often presents us, the Scriptures are highly valued. Many of his characters would agree with the Sandwich Islands lunatic who called the Bible "The precious of the precious— the book of books—the Sacred Scriptures" (*Letters from Hawaii,* 74). Shoveling in a lot of Scripture, as Twain had Brown term it (211), was entirely commonplace in conversation. Even letters were thought better if they could work up some kind of Scriptural climax.[12]

Twain had little patience with such adulation of the Bible and scoffed at what he called "that kind of so-called housekeeping where they have six Bibles and no corkscrew" (*Notebook,* 210). Particularly was he provoked by those who quoted the Bible in the hope of gaining something for themselves. As early as *The Gilded Age* Twain had invented a corporation which sought to gain its illegitimate ends by use of the Bible. The president of the fraudulent Columbus River Slackwater Navigation Company tells Washington Hawkins that a religious paper is a good place for a writeup on their proposed improvement and that the article had better have a few Scripture quotations in it (*Writings,* X, 308).

Twain hated religious hypocrites, whether individuals or nations as a whole. Senator Dilworthy of *The Gilded Age* ranks as one of his finest fictional hypocrites. Just as bad in real life was King Leopold of Belgium, who, though a Christian, was engaged in slaughter and torture of the Congolese. In "King Leopold's Soliloquy," written in 1905, Twain pictured the King as mouthing such pious sayings as "that I might ... lift up those ... blacks out of darkness into light, the light of our blessed Redeemer, the light that streams from his holy Word." At one point Leopold even confesses how he "went pilgriming among the Powers in tears, with my mouth full of Bible and my pelt oozing piety at every pore."[13] An earlier piece, "The Stupendous Procession," made it clear that Twain regarded all Christian nations as guilty of crimes inconsistent with the Bible they profess to revere.[14] The

United States was not spared, either. Of Teddy Roosevelt and an infamous massacre, Twain wrote: "He knew perfectly well that to pen six hundred helpless and weaponless savages in a hold like rats in a trap and massacre them ... would not have been a brilliant feat of arms even if Christian America ... had shot them down with bibles and the Golden Rule instead of bullets."[15]

Another thing to which Twain naturally objected was the way people interpret the Bible. An entire article, "Bible Teaching and Religious Practice"[16] took the Christian church to task for being so slow to change its interpretations of the Bible.[17] It is the world which has to correct the Bible, Twain declared; the church is the last to accept the new interpretation, though it invariably takes the credit for it. As examples Twain cited the preaching of hell and damnation, slavery, witches, and infant damnation. Slavery particularly roused his ire, for he well remembered the sermons he had heard as a boy which proved by the Bible the inferior state of the Negro and the justice of his being in servitude.[18]

Sometimes specific interpretations riled Twain, such as John D. Rockefeller, Jr.'s exposition of "Sell all thou hast and give to the poor" (Luke 18:22). Rockefeller taught his Bible class that the verse did not necessarily mean what it said; its real meaning was that one should remove at any cost whatever obstruction might stand between him and salvation.[19] Nine out of ten clergymen who were asked for their opinions sided with the Rockefeller interpretation, leading Twain to grumble in reference to another matter: "I have never seen such slipshod work, bar the ten that interpreted for the home markets the 'sell all thou hast.' "[20]

Another Rockefeller interpretation to which Twain

objected was that concerning Joseph's financial operations in Egypt, and here Twain's insight was actually
ahead of his time. Rockefeller, along with many ministers
of that day, saw Joseph's actions in Genesis 47 as
entirely fair and reasonable. Twain would not stand
for such "whitewashing." In an autobiographical dictation of 1906, he quoted the passage in question and
supplied his conclusion, that Joseph "skinned them of
every last penny they had, of every last acre they had,
of every last animal they had; then bought the whole
nation's *bodies* and *liberties* on a 'fair market' valua-
tion for bread and the chains of slavery."[21] For Twain
it was another case of people being unable to see the
text for what it really was. Having already made up
their minds about Joseph, they were determined to justify his conduct, no matter how unreasonable it might
really be.[22]

Twain was never the kind of person who stops with
saying that the Bible is being wrongly used or mis-
interpreted. To him the book itself deserved harsh criticism. Others might surround it with a robe of sanctity
and exempt it from the close scrutiny given other
books, but not Twain. Scathingly he enumerated what
seemed to him its major faults.

First, the Bible is not true. It claims to be telling the
truth, and its partisans maintain that it cannot err, yet
to his eye it was filled with lies. Twain regarded the
fall, the flood, and many of the events of the life of
Christ as falsehoods.[23] As early as 1870 he looked upon
the Bible as "a mass of fables and traditions, mere
mythology" (*Biography*, 411). A few years later he
made a similar equation when he wrote Howells that
"most of the facts of life rest only on some one's word
—including the facts of the Scriptures, & the Arabian
Nights & all that kind of books" (*Twain-Howells Let-*

ters, II, 586). This may be supposed a joke, which it was, but it is nevertheless not so far removed from what he really believed.

The main reason Twain refused to accept the Bible as true was the miraculous quality of so many of its narratives and the fact that they could not be verified by one's own experience. Story after story contains violations of natural law unacceptable to many modern minds. In view of the lack of supporting evidence for the Bible's claims that the sun stood still or that Lazarus was raised from the dead, Twain concluded that the only rational position was that these events did not happen. Of course Twain doubted a good many biblical teachings which did not involve miracles. In his autobiographical dictations, for instance, he stated that according to the hearsay evidence of the Bible, God is love, justice, compassion, and forgiveness, but that all the evidence of experience indicated the opposite ("Reflections," 350).

There was a second sense in which Twain believed the Bible contrary to the laws of nature. This is the way he put it in his notebook entry of July 4, 1898, at Kaltenleutgeben, Austria: "There is no law in the Bibles and the Statute Books limiting the appetites and the passions that has any but one function, to wit: to limit the law of God" (*Notebook*, 343). Ten years later he dictated into his autobiography almost the same sentiment, though clarifying his meaning: "I couldn't call to mind a written law of any kind ... in ... any Bible for the regulation of man's conduct in *any* particular, from assassination all the way up to Sabbath-breaking, that wasn't a violation of the law of Nature, which I regarded as the highest of laws, the most peremptory and absolute of all laws—Nature's laws being in my belief plainly and simply the laws of

God" (*Eruption*, 315). The Bible, for example, commands man not to kill, but there is a law of God planted in man's heart at birth which says "Thou shalt kill."[24] For God to give man a nature inclined to killing and then command him not to kill is patently absurd, yet the Bible time and again shows God punishing men merely for obeying the laws of their natures; Adam was the first.[25]

The Bible's lack of originality came under Twain's fire. According to him, "This Bible is built mainly out of the fragments of older Bibles that had their day and crumbled to ruin" (*LE*, 14). He did not really demonstrate the truth of this rather sweeping generalization, but limited himself to affirming the "poverty of invention" noticeable in its "three or four most imposing and impressive events," the golden rule, the flood, and the virgin birth ("Reflections," 355). Returning to generalities, Twain observes that there are only two really new things in the Bible—heaven and hell (*LE*, 14). He seems not to have been aware that writers such as Homer and Plato had depicted places of punishment and reward long before the New Testament was written. Twain obviously was at times an inept and amateurish Bible critic.

A far more serious charge leveled by Twain against the Bible was that it had a pernicious influence on mankind. Not only had its texts condoned slavery (the curse of Canaan, Genesis 9:25) and the execution of witches (Exodus 22:18), but they had also supported unthinkable cruelties committed in the name of Christianity. Indeed, in his more reckless moments, Twain accused the Bible of having drenched the planet in blood ("Reflections," 341–42). Presumably he had in mind the example set by the wholesale slaughter of non-Israelites which God commanded in the Old Testament. He also felt that the Bible contained a good deal of bad counsel, even in the New Testament. Incensed by reading accounts of holy men who, sometimes rather cruelly, broke all ties with family and friends, believing they were doing the will of God, he once wrote in the margin of such an account: "Christ had given ... the most distinct and unmistakable warrant for this belief and this conduct."[26] And he added the comment that "plainly, God never knew anything about human beings or he would not have trusted the idiots with so dangerous a thing as the Bible." Why was it dangerous? Because some people had no better sense than to do whatever it said.

One particular aspect of the Bible's pernicious influence which Twain liked to dwell on was its obscenity. His recollection of having "to read an unexpurgated Bible through before I was 15 years old" was followed by his comment, "none can do that and ever draw a clean sweet breath again this side of the grave" (*Twain's Autobiography*, II, 335–36). In his long-suppressed autobiographical dictations he declared that there had never been a Protestant boy or girl whose mind had not been soiled by the Bible: "The Bible does its baleful work in the propagation of vice among children, and vicious and unclean ideas, daily and constantly, in every Protestant family in Christendom. It does more of this deadly work than all the other unclean books in Christendom put together; and not only more, but a thousandfold more. It is easy to protect the young from those other books, and they are protected from them. But they have no protection against the deadly Bible" ("Reflections," 342). As proof, Twain offered no examples but appealed instead to the reader's own experience. In "Letters from the Earth" he grew bolder, citing a few of the passages which, according to him, children "hunt out and study in private."[27]

The pettiness and cruelty of the Bible God never failed to arouse Twain's anger. That God should have been so small seemed ridiculous to him, and in an essay of 1891 he set forth his idea of the limited view of the Old Testament: "the Deity's possessions consisted of a small sky freckled with mustard-seed stars, and under it a patch of landed estate not so big as the holdings of the Tsar to-day, and all His time was taken up in trying to keep a handful of Jews in some sort of order."[28] By 1906 Twain was denouncing God still more strongly for having chosen a few of the millions of people on the earth, making pets of them, and resolving "to keep and coddle them alone and damn all the rest" ("Reflections," 344). God was not only small in field of vision but in character as well; witness his "I the Lord thy God am a jealous God" (Exodus 20:5; Deuteronomy 5:9). This, Twain asserted, was but another way of saying, "I the Lord thy God am a small God; a small God, and fretful about small things" (*LE*, 27). Perhaps it was disgust with this small deity that led Twain to picture in such extreme terms the vastness and remoteness of that being he termed "the real God."[29]

Twain's disgust at the pettiness of the Bible God was more than matched by his horror at the cruelties ascribed to him. As far back as the *Quaker City* letters he had shown disapproval of the cruelty of such stories as Jael's killing Sisera by driving a tent peg through his temple.[30] But this was nothing compared to his attacks on the cruelty of God himself.

What outraged Twain most about the Bible God was his killing of innocent people as well as guilty. "I knew," he wrote in 1906, "that in Biblical times, if a man committed a sin, the extermination of the whole surrounding nation—cattle and all—was likely to happen. I knew that Providence was not particular about the rest, so that He got somebody connected with the one He was after" (*Eruption*, 261). In "Letters from the Earth" he remarked of Onan's sin that it was hard to understand why God should have been satisfied with punishing Onan alone instead of "slaying all the inhabitants for three hundred miles around—they being innocent of offense, and therefore the very ones he would usually slay. ... If he had a motto, it would have read, 'Let no innocent person escape.' "[31] It was perhaps in his suppressed dictations that Twain became most eloquent in his denunciation of God's cruelty: "He is always punishing—punishing trifling misdeeds with thousandfold severity; punishing innocent children for the misdeeds of their parents; punishing unoffending populations for the misdeeds of their rulers; even descending to wreak bloody vengeance upon harmless calves and lambs and sheep and bullocks as punishment for inconsequential trespasses committed by their proprietors. It [the Old Testament] is perhaps the most damnatory biography that exists in print anywhere" ("Reflections," 332). Twain did not fail to document his charges here. He cited the flood (*LE*, 49) and the plagues of Egypt (*Biography*, 1355–56), as examples of the punishment of the innocent, and his exhibit A was the slaughter of the Midianites, which he related in detail in "Letters from the Earth."[32] Briefly, the story was this: the Israelites made war on the Midianites as God commanded and slew all the males, burning their cities and taking all the booty they could. But the Israelites spared the lives of all the women and children. Moses, angered at this, ordered the deaths of every male child and of every woman that "hath known man by lying with him." The virgins were to be spared for the Israelite men. No one could pretend that it is a pretty story, and Twain bore down heavily on its concept of God: "He slays, slays, slays! All the men, all the beasts, all the boys, all the babies; also all the women and all the girls, except those that have not been deflowered. . . . There is nothing in either savage or civilized history that is more utterly complete, more remorselessly sweeping than the Father of Mercy's campaign among the Midianites" (*LE*, 51–52, 53). The sarcasm of the last sentence becomes more explicit through Twain's reminder to the reader that after all it was God himself who gave the commandment "Thou shalt not kill" (*LE*, 48).

One might have supposed that Twain would like the New Testament a good deal better than the Old, since it presents a much more acceptable concept of God, but this was not the case—at least not in the last ten years of his life. Of course Twain saw that in the New Testament Christ appears as a teacher of morals, gentleness, meekness, righteousness, and purity (*LE*, 54), but he would not ignore what he had read in the Old. Not allowing for progressive revelation, he attacked as if Christians were required to believe everything the Bible said of God, regardless of where it appeared or what its source. In a notebook entry he called the God of the Old and New Testaments "the Jekyl and Hyde of sacred romance" (*Notebook*, 392). The Old Testament, he said in "Letters from the Earth," "gives us a picture of these people's Deity as he was before he got religion, the other one gives us a picture of him as he appeared afterward. The Old Testament is interested mainly in blood and sensuality. The New one in Salvation. Salvation by fire" (*LE*, 44).

86

It was the fire of hell that Twain most objected to in the New Testament. To him it seemed monstrously inconsistent that Jesus should present himself as "sweet, and gentle, merciful, forgiving" and then invent and proclaim hell. This, he thought, made Jesus (or God, since the two were said to be the same) "a thousand billion times crueler than ever he was in the Old Testament" (*LE*, 45). The notion was more fully elaborated in an autobiographical dictation: "The earthly half [of God, i.e. Christ] requires us to be merciful and sets us an example by inventing a lake of fire and brimstone in which all of us who fail to recognize and worship Him as God are to be burned through all eternity. And not only *we*, who are offered these terms, are to be thus burned if we neglect them, but also the earlier billions of human beings are to suffer this awful fate, although they all lived and died without ever having heard of Him or the terms at all. This exhibition of mercifulness may be called gorgeous. We have nothing approaching it among human savages, nor among the wild beasts of the jungle. ... Nothing in all history— nor even His massed history combined—remotely approaches in atrocity the invention of Hell" ("Reflections," 333-34, 335). Contrasting himself with Christ, Twain elsewhere remarked that he had known only three or four men during his lifetime whom he would like to see writhing in flames for even a year, much less forever. Sarcastically he added his doubts that he would even let them burn for a year: "I am soft and gentle in my nature, and I should have forgiven them seventy-and-seven times, long ago."[33] Twain had some Scriptural support for his notion of hell, though he plainly ignored such passages as the scene of the Last Judgment in Matthew 25, where it is not belief in Christ which determines salvation, but one's conduct toward his fellow man. Not even Dante interpreted the punishment of hell so strictly as Twain: he gave the virtuous pagans a relatively light punishment, where Twain would have had them writhing in flames.

Twain's other major point against the New Testament was that its moralities do not match the conduct of God in the Old Testament. In "Letters from the Earth" he quoted eight verses from the Beatitudes, italicizing "Blessed are the merciful" and "Blessed are the peace-makers." Far from praising these verses, he denounced them as "immense sarcasms" and "giant hypocrisies" uttered by the same mouth which ordered the wholesale massacre of the Midianites. The Beatitudes, he said, should be read together with Numbers and Deuteronomy so that Christians can get "an all-round view of Our Father in Heaven" (*LE,* 54–55). For such criticism to be valid, Christ must be completely identified with God, and everything that is stated of God in the Old Testament must be true and not merely the conception of the writer. Twain may have thought that Christians generally believed this, but if he did, he was allowing his early fundamentalist environment to color unduly his image of his audience, a flaw which appears all too often in his attacks on the Bible.

Twain's views of Christ himself appear to have undergone considerable change during the course of his lifetime. In his early letters to Livy and to Mrs. Fairbanks he had spoken of Christ only with reverence, while in an essay of 1871 he had declared: "All that is great and good in our particular civilization came straight from the hand of Jesus Christ."[34] And in 1878 Twain was writing Orion that though he was not divine, Christ was "a sacred Personage" who ought never to be referred to "lightly, profanely, or otherwise than with the profoundest reverence" (*Letters*, I, 323). He is even on record as having said that he would like to write a life of Christ, but he may not have been serious.[35]

Obviously something drastic happened in Twain's thinking about Christ between 1878 and the attacks of 1906 and 1909 which we have reviewed. By his last years he had come to the conclusion that there had not been "a Christ with the character and mission related by the Gospels." To Paine he said: "It is all a myth. There have been Saviors in every age of the world. It is all just a fairy tale, like the idea of Santa Claus" (*Biography*, 1482). There was scarcely any part of Christ's life Twain left uncriticized. His objections to the story of the virgin birth have already been quoted. He denied the historicity of the slaughter of the innocents, pointing out that it was not mentioned by Tacitus and further arguing that no king such as Herod could have ordered the killing of the first born of Roman subjects (*Biography*, 1468–69). The temptation of Christ in the wilderness made no sense to Twain either, especially Satan's promising him the world if he would fall down and worship him: "That was a manifestly absurd proposition, because Christ, as the Son of God, already owned the world; and besides, what Satan showed him was only a few rocky acres of Palestine. It is just as if some one should try to buy Rockefeller, the owner of all the Standard Oil Company, with a gallon of kerosene" (*Biography*, 1469). Twain did not like the stories of miracles performed by Christ for two reasons. First, he thought them false. In his notebook he wrote in 1904: "A miracle is by far the most wonderful and impressive and awe-inspiring thing we can conceive of, except the credulity that can take it at par."[36] A second reason for attacking the miracles supposes that they did occur. If they did, he says, then they are nothing but additional reasons to condemn the unwonted cruelty of Christ: "[He] satisfies Himself with restoring sight to a blind person here and there instead of restoring it to all the blind; cures a cripple here and there instead of curing all the cripples; furnishes to five thousand famishing persons a meal and lets the rest of the millions that are hungry remain hungry. ... He raised several dead persons to life. He manifestly regarded this as a kindness. If it was a kindness it was not just to confine it to half-a-dozen persons. He should have raised the rest of the dead" ("Reflections," 334). As for Christ's teachings, here it must be said that with the exception of the doctrine of hell, Twain thought them excellent, especially the golden rule and "Love thy neighbor as thyself." What disturbed him was that God and Christ did not follow their own injunctions to be merciful and to forgive. There can be no doubt that Twain considered the teachings of the Sermon on the Mount the most significant part of the whole story of Christ.

The fundamentalists of Twain's day thought the teaching of Christ good, but regarded his atoning death on the cross the most significant act of his life. Twain's voice was a dissenting one. In the first place, he professed to see nothing unique in the event: "For men to throw their lives away for other people's sake is one of the commonest events in our everyday history" (*Notebook*, 290). Only a few hours of pain were involved, and that was not much for one with Christ's perspective: "For God to take three days on a Cross out of a life of eternal happiness and mastership of the universe is a service which the least among us would be glad to do upon the like terms" (364). The whole atonement scheme seemed to Twain extremely irrational. As he explained it in his notebook: "If Christ was God, He is in the attitude of One whose anger against Adam has grown so uncontrollable ... that nothing but a sacrifice of life can appease it, and so without noticing how illogical the act is going to be, God condemns Himself to death ... and in this ingenious way wipes off that old score. It is said that the ways of God are not like ours. Let us not contest this point."[37] Once again the fundamentalist Christology strongly influenced Twain with its close identification of Christ with God and its emphasis upon his divinity until his humanity is almost lost sight of. More orthodox Christians might simply write off Twain as a bad theologian for not recognizing that according to the Council of Chalcedon, Christ was fully human and therefore the atonement is not merely a case of God condemning himself.

How much is left of the life of Christ? About as much as was left of Fenimore Cooper's art when Twain finished with it. The virgin birth, the slaughter of the innocents, the temptation in the wilderness, the miracles, the teachings, the crucifixion—objections have been raised to all of these. What is left is important. Perhaps not this time, though, for what is left is obviously the Resurrection. Twain never denied it specifically, very likely because he thought it the most cherished belief of Christians, but to deny it would only be the next logical step after the conclusions we have listed. In fact, when Twain told Paine that the whole story of Christ is a fairy tale of the Santa Claus variety, he was by implication including the Resurrection.

The statement with which this chapter began indicated that there were certain aspects of the Bible which had Twain's approval. By now, however, it must be apparent that to him the bad far outweighed the good. One could cite passages from Twain's writings singling out things that he liked in the Bible, but almost all of them would be from works done before 1880. Even the distance between the biblical fantasies and "Reflections on Religion" is considerable. Professor James D. Williams remarks in connection with *A Connecticut Yankee:* "history was becoming for him almost exclusively a source of material for moral indignation rather than for anachronistic farce. In *A Connecticut Yankee* he increasingly—if by no means consistently—looked for historical examples of cruelty and injustice as the cores for successive narrative episodes. The shift within the *Yankee* itself from farce towards bitter humor and indignation parallels that larger pattern of changing emphasis which characterizes Mark Twain's work in its totality."[38] If the biblical fantasies contain a good deal of anachronistic farce, the attacks on the Bible are certainly charged with moral indignation. Too much so, in fact, for them to have the impact Twain might have wished. Their excesses betray precisely the fault that Twain described to Howells in 1879: "I wish I *could* give those sharp satires on European life which you mention, but of course a man can't write successful satire except he be in a calm judicial good-humor—whereas I *hate* travel and I *hate* hotels, & I *hate* the opera & I *hate* the Old Masters—in truth I don't ever seem to be in a good enough humor with ANYthing to *satirize* it; no, I want to stand up before it & *curse* it, & foam at the mouth,—or take a club & pound it to rags & pulp" (*Twain-Howells Letters,* I, 248). There is a little too much cursing and foaming at the mouth in "Reflections on Religion" and "Letters from the Earth" for them to be really convincing. Twain was unfortunately unable to see any redeeming features in the sections of the Bible over which he pondered so long. The theology of sin, judgment, and grace which modern scholars find in the Yahwist epic (which includes the fall and the flood) was never detected by him. He could see the judgment all right, but not the grace. In his choice of incidents from the Bible Twain more or less followed the principle Professor Williams describes: "He was increasingly interested in finding instances of 'the abyss of depravity into which it is possible for human nature to sink.' "[39] Nothing illustrates this better than the "history of the progress of the human race" presented by Satan in "The Mysterious Stranger" including as it does Cain's murder of Abel, the flood, Noah overcome with wine, Sodom and Gomorrah, the incest between Lot and his daughters, the Hebraic wars, and Jael's murder of Sisera (*Complete Short Stories*, 658). "Letters from the Earth" and "Reflections on Religion" similarly focus almost exclusively on those parts of the Bible which show man and God in the worst light. That these events might not be true was little help; as Twain had Satan say, "If we believe ... that ... God invented these cruel things, we slander him; if we believe that these people invented them themselves, we slander them. It is an unpleasant dilemma in either case" (*LE*, 14). For Twain the Bible was simply one more proof of the stupidity and depravity of "the damned human race."

5.

Conclusion

THE PRESENT generation has discovered a new Mark Twain. No longer is he merely the nostalgic recaller of the past, the teller of tall tales, the producer of humorous quips. No one today would describe him in the terms used by Stuart P. Sherman in his sketch for the *Cambridge History of American Literature:* "Mark Twain is one of our great representative men. He is a fulfilled promise of American life. He proves the virtues of the land and the society in which he was born and fostered. He incarnates the spirit of an epoch of American history when the nation ... entered lustily upon new adventures."[1] Thanks to the posthumous publication of a number of his own works and to the efforts of the many scholars who have directed their attention toward him, we now know that he was a far more complex figure, a man divided against himself almost as much as his "extraordinary twins" whose bedtime reading consisted of *The Age of Reason* and *The Whole Duty of Man.*

Justin Kaplan's Pulitzer prize biography *Mr. Clemens and Mark Twain* contains perhaps the fullest examination of Twain's duality. Beginning with his title,

Conclusion

Kaplan argues that Twain was "a double creature" who "wanted to belong, but he also wanted to laugh from the outside. The Hartford literary gentleman lived inside the sagebrush bohemian."[2] This simultaneous desire to be respectable and yet not be is made thoroughly apparent by a study of Twain's use of the Bible.

A basic duality lies at the heart of Twain's position with regard to the Bible and religion. Although he rejected orthodoxy early in life and nearly always classified himself a "sinner," he nevertheless maintained to the end a great interest in all things having to do with Christianity. Clearly this was so because of the powerful hold which the fundamentalism of his early environment had on his imagination—a hold which John Marshall Clemens, John Quarles, Thomas Paine, Freemasonry, and Robert Ingersoll could not break. Many another man of like belief would have brushed Christianity aside and thought little more about it; few indeed would have let it and its Bible so dominate their thinking and writing. But Twain could no more let go of Christianity than he could his desire to be respected and admired by the reading public.

The nonrespectable side of Twain wished to deride and ridicule the Bible for all it was worth. The impulse to do so appeared as early as 1870 and increased progressively as he grew older and more and more misfortunes overtook him. Although he had little to offer in the way of new ideas or an informed understanding of biblical scholarship, he wished to reveal the book's foolishness and pernicious influence. Furthermore, he wished to expose the hypocrisy of its readers. People generally, he believed, lie about the Bible, deceive themselves about it. Like the pilgrims in the Holy Land, they do not see what is really there but only what someone tells them they should see. Secure in their smug piety, they are often less Christian than persons who have little to do with the church and who know scarcely anything about the Bible. Surely Huck Finn and Jim are more obedient to the commands of the gospel than are the nominally Christian Miss Watson, the Grangerfords and Shepherdsons, or Uncle Silas and Aunt Sally Phelps. Twain again and again in his stories showed false piety being punctured by realistic irreverence or else contrasted with what he considered genuine religion—obedience to the golden rule and the command to love one's neighbor. The Scriptural Panoramist vs. his accompanist, Twain vs. Brown, the pilgrims vs. sinners on the *Quaker City*, the river towns vs. Huck—all show the same basic criticism of "official Christianity."

It must be said, however, that while Twain all along sided with the minority protest group against the genteel majority, he was also on the side of the latter group. The respectable side of his nature realized that the public regarded the Bible and Christianity as sacred, even though they paid little enough attention to their precepts. Twain was thus led to suppress in some manner the more outspoken and extravagant attacks which he made upon religion and particularly upon the Bible. The irreverence of the *Quaker City* letters was toned down for *Innocents Abroad*, a book destined for a national public rather than for readers in San Francisco and New York; the unorthodoxy of "The Turning Point of My Life" was smoothed over with humor and fantasy; manuscripts such as "Captain Stormfield's Visit to Heaven" were filed away for years before being published; the autobiographical dictations of June 1906 were "not to be exposed to any eye until the edition of A.D. 2406." Perhaps Twain remembered the example of Thomas Paine: the nation had much cause to be grateful to the author of *Common Sense* and *The Crisis*, but it refused to grant any honor to the author of *The Age of Reason*. He must have believed that if he wanted the applause of the public—and he certainly did—his course must not be that of Paine, who openly published his unorthodox opinions, but that of Jefferson, who largely concealed his. The so-called Jefferson Bible was first printed in 1904, two years before Twain dictated his "Reflections on Religion," scheduled for publication one to five hundred years later.

At once iconoclast and conformist, Twain sought to shatter the idols of the dominant culture but stood unwilling to be branded an idol-shatterer by that culture. He wished to shock the easily shockable, but not to the point where they would no longer admire him or continue to buy and read his books. In his last years Twain delighted to believe he could shock the public out of its senses if he only would, while at the same time lying secure in the knowledge that he was not going to do it until he was dead. Once when he was keeping from his seriously ill wife the news of the equally serious illness of their daughter Jean, Twain wrote Twichell: "With a word I could freeze the blood in her veins!"[3] That was precisely his position with regard to telling the world the truth about the Bible; in both cases he knew he was not going to speak the word. And so he treated the story of Adam and Eve with humor and sentiment in *Adam's Diary* and *Eve's Diary*, both of which were published shortly after being written, and kept to himself the bitter reflections on the story which appear in *Letters from the Earth* and other posthumous writings.

It must be said, by the way, that in spite of a certain amount of common sense in them, Twain's suppressed attacks on the Bible have all too often a sense of merely blowing off steam. A significant insight into his practice may be gained by examining part of a letter-writing scheme which Twain proposed to Howells: "And you can talk with a quite unallowable frankness & freedom, because you are not going to send the letter. ... As he will never see it, you can make it really indecenter than he [Twichell] could stand; & so no harm is done, yet a vast advantage is gained" (*Twain-Howells Letters*, II, 845). "Letters from the Earth" and "Reflections on Religion" were, one suspects, deliberately made more outrageous than the public could stand. Since 1870, Twain had wanted to write "a perfect lightning-striker," and now he had done it—or so he thought. But no one was to hear the thunder until long after his death. What the "vast advantage" was is hard to say, other than simply getting something off his chest.

Blowing off steam was of course not Twain's only deficiency in his handling of the Bible. Although he uses many apt quotations and references, one can observe a certain laziness in him which is perhaps most obvious in his frequent failure to check the biblical material he incorporated into his writings. At times he did go over it fairly carefully, but he often relied on an imperfect recollection. Besides his imprecise quoting he sometimes made factual errors as well: he identified Barabbas as one of the thieves crucified with Christ,[4] made it the poor who are to inherit the earth instead of the meek,[5] and placed Cain's murder of Abel in the Garden of Eden.[6] Numerous small mistakes, such as adding a final "s" to the book of Revelation,[7] appear. Once made, such a mistake is likely to be repeated time and again. Occasionally an error was corrected only to be resumed a short time later. Laziness also shows in

Twain's tendency to make automatic associations. Noise and confusion inevitably reminded him of the Tower of Babel; a murder, of Cain and Abel; wisdom, of Solomon. Examining Twain's writings over the span of his lifetime reveals that he did tend to use the same device or expression again and again. He apparently reasoned, for instance, that if treating a book of the Bible as if it were a person was funny one time, it should be the fourth or fifth time. Any number of passages might be cited in which Twain fell back on well-tried formulas.

This same lack of originality is also observable in Twain's arraignment of the Bible. His charges were not new, for the most part, though his manner of expressing them may have been. Certainly he did some thinking for himself, but the major points he raised had all been made by Paine or Ingersoll. Twain was, it must be admitted, something of a dabbler in biblical scholarship and perhaps even in Bible reading. There is not much evidence that he had read the Bible systematically; his citations of the Bible could more often than not have come from sermons, conversations, or memories of Sunday school teaching. His use of the first eleven chapters of Genesis is far out of proportion to the importance of that section to the Bible as a whole. Some sections, such as the writings of the Old Testament prophets, he seems to have neglected almost entirely, save for a few impressive phrases from Isaiah. What must surprise the reader more is his apparent failure to comprehend the real content of such books as Job and Ecclesiastes. One would think that their pessimistic and questioning outlook would be made to order for Twain, but he seldom goes beyond the verses in them which pious souls in Hannibal were fond of quoting. In Ecclesiastes, for instance, he often makes use of "Cast thy bread upon the waters: for thou shalt find it after many days" (11:1), but never such verses as the following—all perfect statements of Twain philosophy: "The thing that hath been, it is that which shall be; and that which is done is that which shall be done: and there is no new thing under the sun" (1:9); "Wherefore I praised the dead which are already dead more than the living which are yet alive. Yea, better is he than both they, which hath not yet been, who hath not seen the evil work that is done under the sun" (4:2–3); "All things come alike to all: there is one event to the righteous, and to the wicked; to the good and to the clean, and to the unclean; to him that sacrificeth, and to him that sacrificeth not" (9:2). The book even contains an admonition concerning dress which Twain delighted to follow in his later years: "Let thy garments be always white" (9:8). But for all their similarity to Twain's law of periodical repetition, the Pudd'nhead maxims, and the attacks on Sunday school literature, he never makes reference to these verses. My conclusion is that he did not know them, and that a great many other biblical references in his writings had come by aural rather than visual acquaintance with the Scriptures. Twain's knowledge of the Bible clearly had gaps in it—gaps that he was unwilling to fill.

What has been said of gaps in Twain's knowledge of the Bible may be reiterated with greater emphasis in regard to biblical scholarship. He knew that people were explaining the "six days" of creation as six long periods, and that scientific explanations of the miracles were being formulated, but he did not know a great deal more. The details of higher criticism, which one might have expected him to seize upon, apparently escaped him. He neither used nor discussed its discoveries. Lacking the guidance which biblical scholarship might have provided, Twain overstressed certain of the Bible's shortcomings, being at the same time blind to its virtues. Scorning others for failing to see what is really in the Bible, he committed the same error himself. Worst of all, he became reckless, leaving behind the reason he valued so much and weakening his arguments by basing them on theological assumptions held only by ultrafundamentalists. A literary genius, Twain was but a feeble Bible scholar, for all his pretense of fusing the two.

In order to get material for his attacks on the Bible, Twain mined the book for passages which might be ridiculed as absurd or attacked as cruel or obscene. The writings of his last five years amply attest to his having found a sufficient number of these, primarily in the Old Testament books of history and especially in Genesis. The absurdities of the stories when taken literally attracted Twain, and visions of what would have had to happen for the stories to be literally true alternately amused and outraged him. But Twain found something else in the Bible too: at least three pertinent images of his own life. The first of these, the Prodigal Son, was only temporary. There was a time during his courtship when this parable seemed to Twain a perfect description of the turn his life was taking, away from bohemianism and toward respectability. We do not know what finally happened to the Prodigal of the parable, but in Twain's case the return was not permanent, even though he did continue to hold certain "respectable" goals of prestige and profit for the rest of his life.

A second, more important image was that of the fall of man. Viewed as literal truth, Twain thought the story of Adam and Eve and their being driven from the Garden of Eden patently absurd, declaring that it "must have been invented in a pirate's nursery, it is so malign and childish" ("Reflections," 335). Several times he spelled out its absurdities for the benefit of his future readers, reminding them that the truly guilty party was the only one who escaped punishment. But Twain undeniably found in the story another kind of truth which was anything but absurd. He knew what it was to look back, like Adam, on a golden world which was forever lost. The Prodigal could go home; Adam and Twain could not. Frequently Twain put himself in Adam's place as the contrast between boyhood days in Hannibal or on Uncle John Quarles' farm and the agonies and sorrows of later life weighed on him heavily. There can be little doubt that the Mad Philosopher speaks for Twain when he comments that "the pure and sweet and ignorant and unsordid civilization of Eden was worth a thousand millions" of what he sarcastically terms "our own wonderful civilization" (*LE*, 97). The extraordinary emphasis which Twain gives to Adam surely derives from a perception of this similarity between them. Twain could jokingly refer to Adam as a "blood relative" or "a connection of mine," but the kinship was not all a joke.

The third major image which fascinated Twain was that of Noah and the flood. Here too, the absurdities of the story were made abundantly clear—humorously in "About All Kinds of Ships" and less humorously in "Letters from the Earth." But one gets the impression from the "Papers of the Adam Family" that in his declining years Twain came to see himself as a kind of Noah, warning civilization against its approaching fate. In this collection of documents Twain depicts life before the flood in a way which makes clear his judgment upon the modern world. Once again the Mad

Conclusion

Philosopher speaks for Twain as he tells Eve, "Your civilization has brought the flood. Noah has said it, and he is preparing" (*LE*, 98). The Prodigal, Adam, Noah —all were exiles of a kind, having left the world they had first known. Only the Prodigal could return to what had been. For Adam and for Noah, once the fall and flood had occurred, there could be no going back. It was Mark Twain's despair that he knew his condition to be the same.

Notes

CHAPTER ONE

[1]"Wit-Inspirations of the Two-Year-Olds," *The Writings of Mark Twain*, Author's National Edition, 25 vols. (New York, 1907–1918), XXIV, 216. Hereafter cited as *Writings*.

[2]*Mark Twain: A Portrait* (New York, 1938), 15, 214.

[3]See for example Edward Wagenknecht, *Mark Twain: The Man and His Work*, 3rd ed. (Norman, Okla., 1967), 61–62; Minnie M. Brashear, *Mark Twain, Son of Missouri* (Chapel Hill, 1934), 207–208; and DeLancey Ferguson, *Mark Twain: Man and Legend* (Indianapolis, 1943), 26.

[4]In *Mark Twain's Notebook*, ed. Albert Bigelow Paine (New York, 1935), 191, an entry of 1886, Twain refers to "That Book whose 'every word' He inspired and whose ideas were all his own." Hereafter cited as *Notebook*. In *Letters from the Earth*, ed. Bernard DeVoto (New York, 1962), 14, Satan reports to Michael and Gabriel that the Christian thinks every word of the Bible was dictated by God. Hereafter cited as *LE*.

[5]Albert Bigelow Paine, *Mark Twain: A Biography*, 3 vols. (New York, 1912), 1281. Hereafter cited as *Biography*.

[6]*Mark Twain's Autobiography*, ed. Albert Bigelow Paine, 2 vols. (New York, 1924), II, 214.

[7]*Writings*, XII, 212.

[8]*Traveling with the Innocents Abroad: Mark Twain's Original Reports from Europe and the Holy Land*, ed. Daniel M. McKeithan (Norman, Okla., 1958), 305–306. Hereafter cited as *Traveling*. The passage is somewhat altered in *Writings*, II, 377–78. Only *Innocents Abroad* specifically mentions Sunday school.

[9]*Mark Twain to Mrs. Fairbanks*, ed. Dixon Wecter (San Marino, Calif., 1949), 3. Hereafter cited as *Mrs. Fairbanks*.

[10]*Traveling*, 293; *Writings*, II, 368.

[11]*Traveling*, 185; *Writings*, II, 183–84.

[12]*Traveling*, 248.

[13]*The Complete Essays of Mark Twain*, ed. Charles Neider (Garden City, N. Y., 1963), 413.

[14]*Report from Paradise*, ed. Dixon Wecter (New York, 1952), xiii.

[15]Quoted in Brashear, 128. The article, titled "Oh, She Has a Red Head" and signed "A Son of Adam," appeared in the Hannibal *Journal*, May 13, 1853. Sam considered it "racy humor."

[16]*Mark Twain's Letters in the Muscatine Journal*, ed. Edgar M. Branch (Chicago, 1942), 23.

[17]*Mark Twain's Letters*, ed. Albert Bigelow Paine, 2 vols. (New York, 1917), I, 40. Cp. Matthew 26:39 and Luke 23:24. Hereafter cited as *Letters*.

[18]*The Pattern for Mark Twain's Roughing It: Letters from Nevada by Samuel and Orion Clemens, 1861–1862*, ed. Franklin R. Rogers (Berkeley and Los Angeles, 1961), 29–30.

[19]Quoted in Effie Mona Mack, *Mark Twain in Nevada* (New York, 1947), 225. Cp. Genesis 7:11. Few biblical passages are so often used by Twain as this one. Variously altered it turns up again in *Writings*, II, 133 (see also *Traveling*, 160); in *Mark Twain's Letters to Will Bowen*, ed. Theodore Hornberger (Austin, Texas, 1941), 18; in *Writings*, VII, 23; in *Mark Twain-Howells Letters: The Correspondence of Samuel L. Clemens and William D. Howells, 1872–1910*, ed. Henry Nash Smith and William M. Gibson, 2 vols. (Cambridge, Mass., 1960), I, 381; and in *Biography*, 1300. When a verse struck Twain's fancy, his memory clung to it through the years and pulled it out whenever it was desired.

[20]*Mark Twain of the Enterprise: Newspaper Articles & Other Documents, 1862–1864*, ed. Henry Nash Smith (Berkeley and Los Angeles, 1957), 51. The story of the feeding of the five thousand occurs in all four Gospels.

[21]*Mark Twain, San Francisco Correspondent: Selections from His Letters to the Territorial Enterprise, 1865–1866*, ed. Henry Nash Smith and Frederick Anderson (San Francisco, 1957), 38–40. Cp. Jim's remark to Tom in *Tom Sawyer Abroad*: "You's reskin' us—same way like Anna Nias en Siffira" (*Writings*, XX, 76).

[22]*San Francisco Correspondent*, 41. Acts 5 makes no mention of a thunderbolt; Ananias simply "fell down, and gave up the ghost."

[23]*Mark Twain's Letters from Hawaii*, ed. A. Grove Day (New York, 1966), 237–38. Hereafter cited as *Letters from Hawaii*. Obookia's story is told in *Roughing It*, but this passage does not appear. Cp. Matthew 25:21, 23.

[24]*Republican Letters*, ed. Cyril Clemens (Webster Groves, Mo., 1941), 12–13, gives such a story, written in 1868, in which the "well done" remark comes from another newspaper writer. The more widely known version is at the end of "Riley—Newspaper Correspondent," *Writings*, XIX, 203–204.

[25]*Mark Twain's Speeches*, ed. Albert Bigelow Paine (New York, 1923), 18.

[26]See for example "Some Account of Ye Washoe Canary" in William Wright, *The Big Bonanza* (New York, 1947), 73–74.

[27]Paul Fatout, *Mark Twain in Virginia City* (Bloomington, Ind., 1964), 124.

[28]*Sketches of the Sixties, Being Forgotten Material Now Collected for the First Time from the Californian, 1864–67*, ed. John Howell (San Francisco, 1926), 171. Cp. Matthew 10:29.

[29]See "About Magnanimous-Incident Literature," *Writings*, XX, 330, and "Simon Wheeler, Detective," *Mark Twain's Satires and Burlesques*, ed. Franklin Rogers (Berkeley and Los Angeles, 1967), 377.

[30]*The Complete Short Stories of Mark Twain*, ed. Charles Neider (Garden City, N. Y., 1957), 620.

[31]*Mark Twain: The Development of a Writer* (Cambridge, Mass., 1962), vii.

[32]*Letters from Hawaii*, 166–68. Cp. John 11:35.

[33]Quoted in *Mark Twain, Business Man*, ed. Samuel Charles Webster (Boston, 1946), 87.

[34]*Mark Twain's Travels with Mr. Brown*, ed. Franklin Walker and G. Ezra Dane (New York, 1940), 202–13.

[35]*Travels with Mr. Brown*, 208. For humorous purposes, Twain frequently pretended confusion about the books of the Bible. His customary procedure was to mention books—especially those of the Pentateuch—as if they were persons. Thus Huckleberry Finn says of the king: "he looked that grand and good and pious that you'd say he had walked right out of the ark, and maybe was old Leviticus himself" (*Writings*, XIII,

210). Other examples may be found in *Traveling*, 218, 275; *Letters*, I, 314; *Twain's Autobiography*, I, 342.

CHAPTER TWO

[1]*Traveling*, 310.

[2]See *Traveling*, 107; *Writings*, II, 69. In this instance, a report of his visit to Mars Hill, Twain still fails to copy the quotation exactly. He consistently refused to be scrupulously accurate in his citations.

[3]*Notebook*, 88.

[4]Van Wyck Brooks, *The Ordeal of Mark Twain*, rev. ed. (New York, 1933), 202, 213.

[5]*Traveling*, 305. *Innocents Abroad* mentions Lot's wife but has nothing like this. Note Twain's pretended ignorance in placing Goliath among the patriarchs. For some reason, the Philistine giant always struck Twain as humorous. In another *Alta California* letter we hear of St. Helena's trying to find "Goliah, or Joshua or Exodus, or any of those parties" (*Traveling*, 275; *Writings*, II, 339, with Exodus omitted). In *Innocents Abroad* we hear of the spot where "David and Goliah used to sit and judge the people" (*Writings*, II, 356). Later Tom Sawyer was to name "David and Goliah" as the first two disciples (*Writings*, XII, 57).

[6]*Writings*, II, 245. In *Roughing It* reference is made to "the beautiful story of Joseph and his brethren" (*Writings*, VIII, 71).

[7]*Traveling*, 221–22. The passage does not appear in *Innocents Abroad*. It is interesting that Twain makes nothing of the Bible narrative's confusion as to whether it was the Midianites or the Ishmaelites who sold Joseph into Egypt. Possibly he was so familiar with the story from hearing it in childhood that he did not recognize any confusion. Although in agreement with some of its conclusions, Twain may well have considered the details of higher criticism too troublesome to master and its attacks too limited. He was aware, however, of what he termed "the 'advanced' school of thinkers" who "applied natural laws to the interpretation of all miracles, somewhat on the plan of the people who make the six days of creation geological epochs, and so forth," and he gives a humorous sample of this when Captain Hurricane Jones relates his version of "Isaac and the

prophets of Baal," according to which petroleum and a match really accomplished what generations of readers had supposed was brought about by the fire of God falling from heaven. "There ain't a thing in the Bible but what is true," declares the captain at the conclusion, "all you want is to go prayerfully to work and cipher out how 't was done." See "Some Rambling Notes of an Idle Excursion," *Writings*, XX, 272–76. Cp. I Kings 18.

[8]*Traveling*, 222. Note the implication that Joseph is like a Wall Street speculator. It was to Joseph's financial operations that Twain objected most strongly. In an autobiographical dictation of 1906, he attacked John D. Rockefeller's favorable interpretation of Joseph. See *Mark Twain in Eruption*, ed. Bernard DeVoto (New York, 1940), 85–91.

[9]*Traveling*, 223. Cp. Revelation 12:14—"a time, and times, and half a time."

[10]*Traveling*, 223. Cp. Genesis 44:1–2.

[11]*Traveling*, 223. Although Twain and others use the phrase "weeping and wailing and gnashing of teeth," it never occurs in this form in the Bible. Cp. Matthew 8:12 and 13:42.

[12]*Traveling*, 223. Cp. Genesis 45:14—"And he fell upon his brother Benjamin's neck, and wept; and Benjamin wept upon his neck."

[13]*Traveling*, 224. Cp., for example, II Kings 16:19—"Now the rest of the acts of Ahaz which he did, are they not written in the book of the chronicles of the kings of Judah?"

[14]*Traveling*, 224. "And he fell on his neck" occurs in Genesis 46:29. Twain was able to use the expression seriously in *Writings*, II, 248.

[15]*Traveling*, 224. Considering the context, it is hard to regard this as other than sarcasm, though Louis J. Budd sees it as ending on a safe idea. See his "Mark Twain on Joseph the Patriarch," *American Quarterly*, XVI (Winter 1964), 580.

[16]*Writings*, II, 248. See Budd's article for a good treatment of Twain's handling of Joseph here and elsewhere.

[17]*Traveling*, 202; *Writings*, II, 208, but with the last sentence omitted. Howells thought this bit of fun "delicious impudence." See *My Mark Twain: Reminiscences and Criticisms* (New York, 1910), 109.

[18]*Traveling*, 219. Cp. Judges 11:4.

[19]*Traveling*, 227. This is probably an elaboration of a note-

book entry: "We have seen no country between here and Damascus capable of supporting any such population as one gathers from the Bible" (*Notebook*, 93).

[20]*Traveling*, 214; *Writings*, II, 232. The omission in Judges 18:9–10 is Twain's.

[21]*Traveling*, 215. Twain's comment was greatly modified in *Writings*, II, 232: "Their enthusiasm was at least warranted by the fact that they had never seen a country as good as this."

[22]*Notebook*, 100. Cp. I Kings 17:4–6.

[23]*Traveling*, 217; *Writings*, II, 234. Isaiah 32:2 has "as the shadow of a great rock." Twain could not be exact even when quoting passages he liked very much.

[24]*Writings*, II, 194. Cp. Luke 14:5 and II Corinthians 3:6.

[25]*Traveling*, 279; *Writings*, II, 343.

[26]*Notebook*, 99; *Traveling*, 302–303.

[27]*Traveling*, 317; *Writings*, II, 438–39.

[28]Quoted in *Mrs. Fairbanks*, 29.

CHAPTER THREE

[1]*Mark Twain's Humor: The Image of a World* (Dallas, 1962), 251–54; *Writings*, III, 148–59.

[2]*The Innocent Eye: Childhood in Mark Twain's Imagination* (New Haven, 1961), 122; *Writings*, XV, 273.

[3]Stone, *Innocent Eye*, 224; *Writings*, XVIII, 310–12.

[4]*Writings*, XX, 178. Cp. Genesis 4:9.

[5]According to my figures, which are more indicative than definitive, Adam is mentioned 76 times, Christ, 44; Noah, 34; the Prodigal Son, 28; Eve, 27; Solomon, 27; and Moses, 22. These are the only characters mentioned more than twenty times.

[6]My figures are: Genesis, 295 references; Matthew, 133; Luke, 78; general Old Testament, 47; John, 42; and Matthew-Mark-Luke, 42. These are the only books which are used more than forty times.

[7]*Traveling*, 247. Cp. *Othello*, I, iii.

[8]*Mark Twain, Business Man*, ed. Samuel Charles Webster (Boston, 1946), 97.

[9]Harold Aspiz, "Mark Twain's Reading: A Critical Study," unpublished dissertation (University of California at Los Angeles, 1949), 317. According to Aspiz's count, in the earlier

letters to Mrs. Fairbanks biblical allusions average one to almost every three hundred words.

[10]*Mrs. Fairbanks*, 59–60. Henry Nash Smith finds this letter a "transparent effort to present himself in a better light to the Langdons" in *Mark Twain: The Development of a Writer* (Cambridge, Mass., 1962), 24. Note that all the biblical references are to Luke's account of Jesus' birth; there are none to Matthew's. The only part of the latter which appealed to Twain was, because of its humorous possibilities, Herod's slaughter of the innocents. When, for instance, Twain thought his daughter Susy might have destroyed a manuscript of his, he remarked to Howells, "O for the return of the lamented Herod!" *Mark Twain-Howells Letters: The Correspondence of Samuel L. Clemens and William D. Howells, 1872–1910*, ed. Henry Nash Smith and William Gibson, 2 vols. (Cambridge, Mass., 1960), I, 54.

[11]*Mrs. Fairbanks*, 33. Cp. Luke 15:16. Here, of course, there is a teasing suggestion that Twain is not so eager to reform.

[12]*Mrs. Fairbanks*, 35. Twain had a tendency to call anyone who was returning a prodigal. Invited to attend a banquet for the Society of California Pioneers, members of which had come back to the East, he sent his "good wishes for the Returned Prodigals, and regrets that I cannot partake of a small piece of the fatted calf (rare and no gravy,)" (*Letters*, I, 165).

[13]Quoted in Clara Clemens, *My Father, Mark Twain* (New York, 1931), 15. Cp. II Timothy 4:7.

[14]"The Love Letters of Mark Twain," ed. Dixon Wecter, *Atlantic Monthly*, CLXXX (November 1947), 38.

[15]*The Love Letters of Mark Twain*, ed. Dixon Wecter (New York, 1949), 105.

[16]*Love Letters*, 134. Cp. Psalm 8:4. It is from this passage that Twain took the title for his deterministic *What Is Man?* (1906).

[17]The marriage inspired a number of puns on the verse "they twain shall be one flesh" (Matthew 19:5 and Mark 10:8), so many that by 1872 Twain remarked: "When a stranger says to me ... some gentle, innocuous little thing about 'Twain and one flesh' ... I don't try to crush that man into the earth—no. I feel like saying: 'Let me take you by the hand, sir; let me embrace you; I have not heard that pun for weeks.' " *Mark Twain's Speeches*, ed. Albert Bigelow Paine (New York, 1923)

37–38. Twain himself once punned on the verse, asking Livy, "are not we Twain one flesh?" (*Mrs. Fairbanks,* 73). Perhaps the most celebrated "Twain" pun was that of Edward Burlingame in Hawaii in 1866; young Burlingame told Twain he was under a scriptural command to accompany him on a walk, proving it by citing Matthew 5:41, "whosoever shall compel thee to go a mile, go with him twain" (*Notebook,* 22; *Biography,* 288).

[18]*Biography,* 411. I believe that the evidence shows Twain's orthodoxy reached its zenith in late 1868 and early 1869 and was already declining before his marriage. Twain's words to Livy recall a similar speech which Paine reports having been made to Rev. Joseph H. Twichell some eight years later: "I don't believe one word of your Bible was inspired by God any more than any other book. I believe it is entirely the work of man from beginning to end—atonement and all. The problem of life and death and eternity and the true conception of God is a bigger thing than is contained in that book" (*Biography,* 631). The truth of the story has been doubted, but the ideas Twain is quoted as having expressed were unquestionably his. For the state of Twain's beliefs about the Bible in the year of his marriage, see *Biography,* 411–12.

[19]*Writings,* XIII, 346. Twain's fiction here is that Tom is merely writing poor English, but the real intent is clear.

[20]Reprinted in *Mark Twain, Son of Missouri,* by Minnie M. Brashear (Chapel Hill, 1934), 118, 128.

[21]*Letters from Hawaii,* 31; *Writings,* VIII, 208.

[22]*Traveling,* 36; *Writings,* I, 204.

[23]*Writings,* II, 338; see also *Traveling,* 273. Note that in the former passage Twain follows Bishop Ussher's chronology, making the creation of Adam occur 6,000 years ago. Deviation from this will shortly be seen.

[24]*Report from Paradise,* ed. Dixon Wecter (New York, 1952), 61.

[25]*The Complete Essays of Mark Twain,* ed. Charles Neider (Garden City, N.Y., 1963), 413–14.

[26]*Sam Clemens of Hannibal* (Boston, 1952), 220. Albert E. Stone similarly comments that "for all practical purposes, his impression of Tom is as infant Adam living ... 'in an eternal summer before the Fall'" (75–76). Note also the narrator's statement in "The Mysterious Stranger," one version of which

is set in Hannibal: "Eseldorf was a paradise for us boys." *The Complete Short Stories of Mark Twain*, ed. Charles Neider (Garden City, N.Y., 1963), 600.

[27]Quoted in Wecter, *Sam Clemens*, 63.

[28]*Twain-Howells Letters*, II, 533–34. In another backward-looking mood he wrote: "Life was a fairy-tale, then, it is a tragedy now" (*Letters*, II, 787).

[29]*Mark Twain's Letters to Will Bowen*, ed. Theodore Hornberger (Austin, Texas, 1941), 27.

[30]Quoted in Hamlin Hill, "The Composition and Structure of *Tom Sawyer*," *American Literature*, XXXII (January 1961), 386. Twain intended at one time that the Connecticut Yankee should make a similar discovery upon his return to England in the nineteenth century, finding all that was "fresh & new" now "changed & become old, so old!" See Roger B. Salomon, "Realism as Disinheritance: Twain, Howells and James," *American Quarterly*, XVI (Winter 1964), 539.

[31]"A Monument to Adam," *Writings*, XXIV, 234. This account of the project was written in 1906.

[32]"The Adam Monument Petition," in *Biography*, 1648–49. Paine dates the petition October 1879 (see also 708). Here Twain adheres to Ussher's chronology.

[33]*Speeches*, 94. Paine says the speech was delivered c. 1880–1885.

[34]*Speeches*, 95, 96. The Pudd'nhead maxim most closely resembling this statement reads: "Whoever has lived long enough to find out what life is, knows how deep a debt of gratitude we owe to Adam, the first great benefactor of our race. He brought death into the world" (*Writings*, XIV, 30).

[35]For details about the various publications of the *Diary*, see Merle Johnson, *A Bibliography of Mark Twain* (New York, 1935), 80–81. According to Johnson the original version and at least one printing of the *Diary* contain no mention of Niagara Falls.

[36]This publication was in *The $30,000 Bequest and Other Stories* (not identical with the volume of that title in the Author's National Edition). Johnson says this text has been slightly revised from that of 1893. The 650 words of new material are in all probability the section of *Eve's Diary* headed "Extract from Adam's Diary." See Johnson, 80–81. A short paragraph headed "Extract from Adam's Diary" appeared at

the conclusion of Twain's essay "Dr. Loeb's Incredible Discovery." Here, however, Twain's major interest was the denunciation of all consensuses, and he merely used Adam as a device to make his point. See *Europe and Elsewhere*, ed. Albert Bigelow Paine (New York, 1923), 308–309. Hereafter cited as *Europe*.

[37]*Writings*, XXIV, 310. To Paine, this was "perhaps the most tenderly beautiful line he ever wrote" (*Biography*, 1225).

[38]Twain's figure of 300,000 years is fifty times the age of the earth as calculated by Ussher.

[39]*Europe*, 339–46. Not dated by Paine, but probably c. 1905.

[40]*Mark Twain's Autobiography*, ed. Albert Bigelow Paine, 2 vols. (New York, 1924), I, 83. The ancestor Twain probably had in mind was his mother, who had once defended Satan, arguing that he had the clearest right of anyone to have the prayers of every Christian (*Twain's Autobiography*, I, 116–17).

[41]*Writings*, XXII, 252. The germ of this passage is contained in an 1898 notebook entry (*Notebook*, 343).

[42]*Writings*, XXIV, 237–38. An editorial note revealed the more common pseudonym of the correspondent signing himself "Satan."

[43]The reader should recall that in the diaries the command is understood by Adam and Eve.

[44]Once again, Twain contradicts the diaries of Adam and Eve. In the latter Eve says, as we have noticed, that she could give up a moon she found in the daytime because she would be afraid someone might be looking. Why should she be afraid if she did not have some idea that she was doing wrong? It seems apparent that she had the moral sense. Incidentally, one might well wonder how someone *could* be looking, while she and Adam were the only persons in the world.

[45]*Europe*, 347–50. Paine does not date it but places it and the items which accompany it between pieces dated 1904 and 1908. 1905 or 1906 seems to me a reasonable date for it and "That Day in Eden."

[46]Twain frequently contradicted himself as to whether sex existed before the fall. In *Adam's Diary*, Cain is not born until a year after Adam and Eve eat the fruit. "That Day in Eden," however, makes it clear that Eve had at least one child before the fall (*Europe*, 343), while "Eve Speaks" records that both Cain and Abel and at least one other child were born while their parents were still innocent and in Eden. In later writings,

Twain went back to the notion that sex came only after the fall. See *LE*, 17. As a further discrepancy, note that in *Adam's Diary* Abel is still alive over ten years after Adam and Eve leave Eden, while in "Eve Speaks" he is dead only three months after their departure. Such details were of little consequence to Twain, it appears. In Genesis, of course, the matter of the time of the births is quite clear: Cain was not born until after Adam and Eve left Eden (Genesis 3:24, 4:1). Whether sex existed prior to the fall is less clear; scholars customarily regard the biblical discrepancy on this point as the result of the combining of two strands of material, one seeing sex as ordained by God from the beginning and the other regarding it as a consequence of the fall.

⁴⁷See *LE*, 76; the work appears in *LE*, 75–92.

⁴⁸*LE*, 81–82. The whole business of carnivorous animals eating vegetables may have come from some of the Bible commentaries of the day. Dan Beard, the illustrator of *A Connecticut Yankee*, told of Twain's delight at seeing a commentary on the flood which related that the meat-eating animals aboard the ark became vegetarians for the duration of the voyage. Twain, so Beard reported, thought it quite funny to imagine a Barbary lion crying, "Noah! Noah! Bring me a bale of hay." See *Hardly a Man Is Now Alive: The Autobiography of Dan Beard* (New York, 1939), 340–41. The notion of vegetarianism also appears in *Paradise Lost*, X, 710–12.

⁴⁹*Traveling*, 170–71; *Writings*, II, 152–53.

⁵⁰*Traveling*, 186; *Writings*, II, 185.

⁵¹Cp. Genesis 7:11, which actually says "were all the fountains of the great deep broken up."

⁵²From the lecture, "The Sandwich Islands," first delivered in 1866. Quoted in *Biography*, 1603. Cp. *Writings*, VIII, 315.

⁵³*The Forgotten Writings of Mark Twain*, ed. Henry Duskis (New York, 1963).

⁵⁴Reproduced in Milton Meltzer, *Mark Twain Himself: A Pictorial Biography* (New York, 1960), 101. One line of the menu reads: "Cold Ham, *also* Shem and Japhet."

⁵⁵*Forgotten Writings*, 140. Cp. Genesis 16:12, Matthew 3:7, and Luke 3:7.

⁵⁶Quoted in *Mrs. Fairbanks*, 118.

⁵⁷*Letters*, II, 488. In this letter Twain erroneously states that he began the Noah's Ark book in Edinburgh in 1873.

[58]*Biography*, 419. In 1909 Twain described it as a less ambitious work: "a Diary, which professed to be the work of Shem, but wasn't" (*Letters*, II, 488). Since there were only eight human beings aboard the ark, it may be that Twain intended to let each have his say. At any rate, he gave Paine that impression.

[59]*Biography*, 419. The excerpts appear on 419–20. Twain seems to have been aware of a fact not explicitly mentioned in the Bible but one which becomes apparent with a little calculating, that Methuselah was alive in the year of the flood. That he was conscious of the biblical chronology appears from his having Shem mention Noah's six hundredth birthday, for Genesis 7:11 records that the flood came in the six hundredth year of Noah's life. In *Letters from the Earth* DeVoto printed an "Extract from Shem's Diary of 920 A.C.," dating it 1907 or 1908. This is almost certainly Twain's resumption of the original "Shem's Diary" of 1870. The chronology (except for the date in the title, which may have been supplied by DeVoto) and treatment in the two are similar.

[60]*Writings*, XXI, 468–73. The sketch was first published in 1893.

[61]Robert Ingersoll, a celebrated infidel much admired by Twain, made a similar point in his lectures. See *The Works of Robert G. Ingersoll*, 12 vols. (New York, 1915), II, 149–50.

[62]Presumably the "cargo list" was Genesis 6:19–20. What Adam says here runs contrary to the passage on the brontosaurus in *Eve's Diary*, a discrepancy resulting from differing purposes in the two writings.

[63]*LE*, 25. Cp. Twain's Sandwich Island picture of the last to die in the flood (*Biography*, 1603).

[64]*LE*, 74. Twain was violating the Genesis chronology here, since it appears that God did not form his plan to destroy mankind until the time of Noah, who was not born until 1056 A.C., over three hundred years after Methuselah was supposed to be writing.

[65]*LE*, 110. The story referred to appears in all four gospels, but only Matthew and Mark use the term "moneychangers."

[66]Adam is now supposed to be in failing health and retired from public activity; in fact, at one point the reader is told that he is dead. He is mentioned as the originator of certain sayings, including "Respectability butters no parsnips" and "Patriotism

is the last refuge of a scoundrel" (*LE*, 93, 103).

[67]In choosing 920 A.C. as the year of the flood, Twain contradicted the biblical chronology, which places that event in 1656 A.C. In Twain it appears that Adam and Eve (or at least Eve, if Adam is really dead) will perish in the flood. In Genesis they had been dead for over seven hundred years when the flood came. Both were alive, however, in 920, or at least Adam was, for it is recorded that he died in 930 A.C. Such a death date would have been impossible in Twain's chronology, for it would have necessitated Adam's being aboard the ark. The dates given here are not stated as such in Genesis, but may be readily calculated from Genesis 5 and 6.

[68]That Twain could still deal humorously with the Bible in this period may be seen from a 1907 letter to a young friend which contains some of the wildest biblical confusion that ever came from his pen: "There, now—*all* your statements have fallen by the wayside like the tares that were sown in Sodom and Gomorrah by David and Goliath and took not root because the ram's horns of Jericho blew them on the wings of the morning to the uttermost parts of the sea." See *Mark Twain's Letters to Mary*, ed. Lewis Leary (New York, 1961), 112–13. Six biblical elements are woven together in this passage: the parable of the sower, the parable of the wheat and the tares, the destruction of Sodom and Gomorrah, David and Goliath, the fall of Jericho, and Psalm 139.

CHAPTER FOUR

[1]On this point I am inclined to agree with DeLancey Ferguson, *Mark Twain: Man and Legend* (Indianapolis, 1943), 126, as opposed to Paine, *Notebook*, 94, and Edward Wagenknecht, *Mark Twain: The Man and His Work*, 3rd ed. (Norman, Okla., 1967), 62.

[2]"Important Correspondence," *Sketches of the Sixties, Being Forgotten Material Now Collected for the First Time from the Californian, 1864–1867*, ed. John Howell (San Francisco, 1926), 174–75.

[3]*Traveling*, 217; *Writings*, II, 234.

[4]"Concerning the Jews," *Writings*, XXII, 274.

[5]*Mark Twain's Satires and Burlesques*, ed. Franklin R. Rogers (Berkeley and Los Angeles, 1967) 432–37.

[6]*Mark Twain: Pilgrim from Hannibal* (New York, 1946), 202.

[7]"The Victorious Bible," *Outlook*, LI (May 25, 1895), 864–65. Originally delivered as a sermon in Twichell's Asylum Hill Congregational Church, Hartford, Connecticut.

[8]*Mark Twain-Howells Letters: The Correspondence of Samuel L. Clemens and William D. Howells, 1872–1910*, ed. Henry Nash Smith and William Gibson, 2 vols. (Cambridge, Mass., 1960), II, 595–96.

[9]*Twain-Howells Letters*, II, 811. On the title pages of two of the dictations Twain wrote: "Not to be exposed to any eye until the edition of A.D. 2406. S. L. C."

[10]See the comments of a number of prominent clergymen in material distributed by United Press International appearing in the Louisville *Courier-Journal* and other newspapers, October 6, 1963. The dictations appeared as "Reflections on Religion," ed. Charles Neider, *Hudson Review*, XVI (Autumn 1963), 329–52. Portions had been previously printed in *Biography*, 1354–57, but inexactly and with unacknowledged omissions.

[11]Paine quotes Twain as saying about this time: "In some details that Old Bible God is probably a more correct picture than our conception of that Incomparable One that created the universe. ... For that Supreme One is not a God of pity or mercy" (*Biography*, 1356).

[12]See for example the model letter in "Simon Wheeler, Detective," *Satires and Burlesques*, 355.

[13]*Mark Twain: Life As I Find It*, ed. Charles Neider (Garden City, N. Y., 1961), 275.

[14]The float labeled "Christendom" has on it a woman holding a slingshot in one hand and in the other a Bible open to the golden rule. Also on the float is a banner inscribed "Love your Neighbor's Goods as Yourself." The German float has a helmeted figure with mailed fist holding aloft a Bible followed by one in chains labeled "Shantung." See Philip S. Foner, *Mark Twain, Social Critic* (New York, 1958), 285, 286.

[15]*Mark Twain's Autobiography*, ed. Albert Bigelow Paine, 2 vols. (New York, 1924), II, 192. The passage relates to the killing of the Moros. A couple of pages later Twain remarks that for the soldiers "it was a long and happy picnic with nothing to do but sit in comfort and fire the Golden Rule into those people down there" (194).

[16]First published in *Europe*, 387–93.

[17]Twain does not seem to me entirely consistent on the question of how much progress Christians have made toward liberalizing their interpretations of the Bible. In "Letters from the Earth" he made it appear that Christians were still the same literalists they had always been, but he gave a different picture in "Aix, the Paradise of the Rheumatics" (1891): "Mighty has been the advance of the nations and the liberalization of thought. A result of it is a changed Deity, a Deity of dignity and sublimity proportioned to the majesty of His office and magnitude of His empire, a Deity who has been freed from a hundred fretting chains and will in time be freed from the rest by the several ecclesiastical bodies who have these matters in charge" (*Europe*, 98).

[18]In his autobiography Twain speaks of those who beat the slave's "handful of humane defenders with Bible texts and billies" (*Twain's Autobiography*, II, 11).

[19]*Mark Twain in Eruption*, ed. Bernard DeVoto (New York, 1940), 85.

[20]*Writings*, XXV, 250-51. See also Twain's remarks on the "Sell all" discussion, 190-93, 196. He does not mention Rockefeller's name, but it is clearly he Twain is speaking of.

[21]*Eruption*, 91. See the entire account, 85-91.

[22]Today Christian scholars are more inclined to agree with Twain than Rockefeller. Walter Russell Bowie, in his exposition of Genesis 47 for *The Interpreter's Bible* (Nashville and New York, 1952), I, 809-12, comments that "this chapter is an illustration of the fact that the actions of even the best men of the Old Testament are not to be praised indiscriminately, as though they were sacrosanct," which is precisely Twain's point.

[23]*Eruption*, 385; "Reflections," 332, 335-36; *Biography*, 1481-82.

[24]*LE*, 48. See also "In the Animals' Court," *LE*, 216-17.

[25]For other expressions of Twain's view of the Bible as opposed to the inner law of man, see *The Autobiography of Mark Twain*, ed. Charles Neider (New York, 1959), 307, and "The Turning Point of My Life," *Complete Essays*, 484.

[26]Chester Davis, "Mark Twain's Religious Beliefs as Indicated by Notations in His Books," *Twainian*, XIV (November-December 1955), 4. No doubt Twain had in mind a passage such as Matthew 10:35-39, beginning, "For I am come to set a

man at variance against his father, and the daughter against her mother. ... He that loveth father or mother more than me is not worthy of me."

²⁷*LE*, 50–51. On the Bible's obscenity see also 42 and *Letters*, II, 805.

²⁸"Aix, the Paradise of Rheumatics," *Europe*, 97.

²⁹Twain's best descriptions of the "real God" are in *Notebook*, 360–62, and "Reflections," 343–45.

³⁰*Traveling*, 220; considerably modified in *Writings*, II, 237. Twain again brings up the story in "The Mysterious Stranger," *Complete Short Stories*, 658.

³¹*LE*, 49. For Onan, see Genesis 38.

³²*LE*, 46–48. Twain here quotes the Bible at great length—perhaps at greater length than anywhere else in all his writings. Strangely, he numbers the verses but does not identify the books or chapters from which they are taken (Numbers 31 and Deuteronomy 20). The quotation is exact, even to the reproduction of the King James italics. Since Twain never manages to be so precise anywhere else, it may be that he had someone copy the passage for him.

³³"As Concerns Interpreting the Deity," *Complete Essays*, 528. To drive home his point, Twain introduces Christ's words from Matthew 18: 21–22, but he gets them wrong. Christ said "seventy times seven," not "seventy and seven." The same mistake appears in *LE*, 19, but Twain has it right in "Reflections," 334.

³⁴"The Indignity Put Upon the Remains of George Holland by the Rev. Mr. Sabine," in *Biography*, 1625. Originally in *Galaxy*, February 1871.

³⁵Paul Blouet, *Jonathan and His Continent* (New York, 1889), 107–108.

³⁶*Notebook*, 393. Two other versions of this thought follow in the notebook. For another attack on miracles, see "Official Report to the I. I. A. S.," *LE*, 147–51. The initials stand for Indianapolis Institute of Applied Science; the report's main point was that "if it is a Miracle, any sort of evidence will answer, but if it is a Fact, proof is necessary" (149).

³⁷*Notebook*, 290. In a dictation of 1907, Twain spoke in highly orthodox fashion of Christ's having "delivered up His life on the cross for the redemption of the human race" (*Erup-

tion, 343). But he was being orthodox only for the moment, or expressing the beliefs of others.

[38]"The Use of History in Mark Twain's *A Connecticut Yankee*," *PMLA*, LXXX (March 1965), 110.

[39]Williams, 103.

CHAPTER FIVE

[1](New York, 1918–1921), III, 1.

[2](New York, 1966), 18.

[3]Quoted in *The Autobiography of Mark Twain*, ed. Charles Neider (New York, 1959), 399.

[4]*Sketches of the Sixties, Being Forgotten Material Now Collected for the First Time from the Californian, 1864–1867*, ed. John Howell (San Francisco, 1926), 143; see also a *Territorial Enterprise* passage reprinted in Edgar M. Branch, *The Literary Apprenticeship of Mark Twain* (Urbana, Ill., 1950), 253.

[5]"Origins of Illustrious Men," *The Complete Humorous Sketches and Tales of Mark Twain*, ed. Charles Neider (Garden City, N.Y., 1961), 82.

[6]"The Mysterious Stranger," *The Complete Short Stories of Mark Twain*, ed. Charles Neider (Garden City, N. Y., 1963), 658. *A Tramp Abroad*, *Writings*, IV, 279, places Cain's altar in Eden.

[7]*Mark Twain, Business Man*, ed. Samuel Charles Webster (Boston, 1946), 105; *Traveling*, 307, and elsewhere.

Index

Abel, 29, 46, 48, 58, 59, 61, 93, 98, 99, 114n46, 115n46
Abelard and Heloise, 25
"About All Kinds of Ships," 65–66, 67, 102
Acts, 8
Adam: studied in Sunday school, 4; red hair, 5; as "old Adam," 17; tomb of, 23–24, 40; general familiarity with story of, 30; Twain's use of and identification with, 31, 40–61, 97, 102–103; proposal to build monument to, 44–45; could not disobey law of his nature, 82; God's anger against, 91; frequency of mention, 30, 110n5; in notes, 112–17 *passim*. *See also Adam's Diary*, "Adam's Soliloquy," "Papers of the Adam Family"
"The Adam Monument," 44–45
Adam's Diary, 45–49, 50, 51, 53, 58, 59, 71, 97, 113n35, 114n46, 115n46
"Adam's Soliloquy," 54, 66–67
Adventures of Huckleberry Finn. See Huckleberry Finn
The Adventures of Tom Sawyer. See Tom Sawyer
The Age of Reason (Thomas Paine), 94, 97
"Aix, the Paradise of Rheumatics," 119n17
Alta California. See San Francisco

American Bible Society, 12–13
The American Claimant, 74
Ananias, the liar, 8, 106n21, 107n22
Ananias: and St. Paul, 20
Arabian Nights, 80
Aspiz, Harold, 111n9
Asylum Hill Congregational Church (Hartford, Conn.), 118n7
Atonement: Twain's rejection of doctrine of, 90–91, 112n18
"Aunt Polly," 42

Baal, 108–109n7
Babel, Tower of, 99
Balaam's ass, 16
Barabbas, 98
Beard, Daniel, 115n48
Beatitudes, 88, 98
Beecher, Henry Ward, 15
Benjamin, 19
Bethlehem, 35–36
Bible: Twain's early acquaintance with, 3, 83; at his Sunday school, 3–4; favorite passages from, 22, 34–35, 74; attitude toward, 73; admiration for style of, 73–74; favorable statement concerning, 74; not true, 80–81; contrary to laws of nature, 81–82; lack of originality, 82; pernicious influence, 82–84; obscenity of, 83–84; pettiness and cruelty of its God, 84–86; discrepancy be-

Index

of, 54, 59, 61–70; simplicity of
style in, 74; lack of originality
of, 82; demonstrates cruelty of
God, 85; indicative of human
depravity, 93; humorous use
of, 107n35
Freemasonry, 13, 95

"Gabriel," 60
Garth, John, 42
Genesis, 13, 80, 82; frequency of
mention, 30, 99, 110n6; doubts
about truth and authority of,
38; quoted, 56; chronology of,
116n59, 116n64, 117n67. *See
also* Adam, Creation, Eden,
Eve, Fall of man, Flood story,
God, Joseph, Noah
Gideon, 24
The Gilded Age, 78
God: distinction between real
and Bible God, 76, 118n11;
pettiness and cruelty of, 76,
84–86; contrast between Old
and New Testament God, 86;
insufficiency of usual concept
of, 112n18; changing beliefs
about, 119n17
Golden rule, 74, 82, 90, 96,
118n14, 118n15
Goliath: studied at Sunday
school, 4; humorous use of, 17,
108n5, 117n68; parallel with
Twain story, 29
Gomorrah. *See* Sodom and Go-
morrah
Good Samaritan. *See* Parables
Goodman, Joe, 39
"Grangerford family," 96
Grimes, William C., writer on
Holy Land, 26

Hall, Fred J., 45
Ham, 63–64, 65
"Hank Morgan": parallel with
Joseph, 29; parallel with other
Twain writings, 68, 69, 113n30
Hannibal, Missouri: Sunday
school at, 3–4, 40–41; work for
newspaper in, 4–5, 40; as Eden,

41–43, 102, 112–13n26; as set-
ting for Satan stories, 55,
113n26
Harper's Magazine, 55
Harper's Weekly, 55
Hartford, Connecticut, 37,
118n7; Twain's house there,
43–44
Hawaii. *See* Sandwich Islands
Hawks, Bishop, 9–10
Heaven, 82
St. Helena, 108n5
Hell: objections to doctrine of,
77, 87–88; preaching of, 79;
originality of, 82
Herod, King of Judea, 89,
111n10
Higher criticism of Bible,
99–100, 108n7
Holy Land: early notions of, 4;
Twain's visit to, 15–28; pil-
grims in, 95–96
Homer, 82
Honolulu, 12
Howells, William Dean, 42, 75,
80, 92, 98, 109n17, 111n10
Huckleberry Finn, 1, 31, 43, 96,
107
"A Humane Word from Satan,"
55

"If I Could Be There," 76
Immaculate conception, 76
"Important Correspondence ...,"
9–10
Indian Summer (Howells), 42
"The Indignity Put Upon the
Remains of George Holland
...," 88
Ingersoll, Robert G., 95, 99,
116n61
"Injun Joe," 42
The Innocents Abroad, 4, 14,
15–28 *passim,* 39, 40, 45, 54, 63,
75, 96, 108n5, 110n21
Is Shakespeare Dead? 40–41
Isaac: humorously mentioned as
book, 13; confused with Elijah,
108–109n7
Isaiah, 22, 74

Index